SOLANO
COMMUNITY COLLEGE

Donation by

SCC President & Governing
Board

The Art
of Hiring
in America's
Colleges &
Universities

Frontiers of Education

Series Editor: Ronald H. Stein

The Art of Hiring in America's Colleges & Universities

edited by Ronald H. Stein & Stephen Joel Trachtenberg

Prometheus Books • Buffalo, New York

Published 1993 by Prometheus Books

97 96 95 94 93   5 4 3 2 1

Library of Congress Cataloging-in-Publication Data

The art of hiring in America's colleges and universities / edited by Ronald
H. Stein and Stephen Joel Trachtenberg.
        p.   cm. — (Frontiers of education)
    Includes bibliographical references.
    ISBN 0-87975-786-8 (alk. paper)
    1. College teachers—Selection and appointment—United States.
2. College personnel management—United States. I. Stein, Ronald H.
II. Trachtenberg, Stephen Joel. III. Series.
LB2332.72.A78   1993
378.1′2—dc20   92-42892
                                                                   CIP

Contents

Preface

Two concerns inspired this book. First, it is the outcome of years of experience of seeing searches take place at all levels within America's colleges and universities, some handled well, some not so well. Second, it is the expression of a long-felt desire to document why some searches are so successful while others are not.

Our approach has been to find experts who have looked in detail at issues in the hiring process and to ask them not only to write scholarly essays, but also to provide the reader with practical suggestions from their own insights and observations.

The Art of Hiring in America's Colleges and Universities is general enough to be used for any search; for all levels and all types of positions. We hope that our efforts will help the reader select the best candidate and, given the rightness of the fit, retain that person at the institution for a number of years. This will pay added benefits since today's financial constraints have made it imperative that we rationalize the cost of searches by increasing the probability that the initial search will be successful.

Above all, we have enjoyed the challenges of developing this book not merely as a useful informal guide, but also as a means of sharing anecdotal material and humorous experiences. We believe it will fulfill the need that both of us have experienced in our professional lives. We truly anticipate that from these pages the reader will glean that which is helpful and relevant for our times.

7

A number of people have given us invaluable help in this project and we wish to acknowledge them. We are indebted to Dr. Arthur Levine at the Harvard University Graduate School of Education for his assistance in suggesting authors for the different chapters. We are, of course, thankful to the contributing authors themselves whose collective efforts have brought our shared labors to fruition. Thanks also to Dr. Henry Ebel for his constructive comments. At the University at Buffalo, Julie Randall and Lalita Subrahmanyan provided research and editorial assistance, and Susan-Marie Fonzi gave us secretarial help. We are grateful to Ruby Calkins at the George Washington University for her efforts in proofreading the galleys and to Mary A. Read and Steven L. Mitchell of Prometheus Books for their help in copyediting the manuscript.

Ronald H. Stein
Buffalo, New York

Stephen Joel Trachtenberg
Washington, D.C.

February 1993

1

Introduction
Understanding the Problem

Ronald H. Stein

American colleges and universities are facing their most difficult
challenge since World War II in finding qualified faculty to teach
our students and administrators to manage and lead our institutions
of higher education. And yet, our institutions are vastly inexperienced and untrained in the art of identifying, recruiting, and hiring
faculty and administrators.

Hiring at institutions of higher education is normally done by
amateurs, through search committees, and the results are often a
matter of serendipity or happenstance. There is seldom a plan, seldom
leadership, seldom a concerted effort. Consequently, the general result is that when an outstanding candidate is brought to the attention
of the search committee, the first question raised is, "Why does
somebody that good want to come to our institution?" It becomes
a variation of Groucho Marx's quip, "I wouldn't want to join any
club that would have me as a member!"

The search committee only compounds its problems during later
stages of the hiring process. The interview becomes a forum for telling

the candidate everything that is wrong with the institution and for airing all the grievances the members of the search committee have against the institution. It would appear to a casual observer that their charge was to do their very best to talk the candidate out of coming to their institution. William J. Hynes (1990) tells of the problem a small science department in a liberal arts college had in hiring a faculty member for a tenure-track position. It seems that while a number of searches had produced excellent candidates, in the end each one refused the department's offer.

> Everyone was puzzled. It turned out that the chair had a very low image of the college and every time he was alone with a candidate he rattled through his list of reasons why a bright, young scientist would not be interested in coming to this college. Each candidate assumed that the chair was imparting a less-than-subtle message not to become serious about the institution. When a new chair assumed leadership in the department, the next search was successful. (p. 58)

Unfortunately, few seem able to recognize that the confusion and potential misunderstanding surrounding the hiring process serve only to undermine its purpose. We persist in paying little attention to how we recruit even though research (Harris and Fink 1987) has shown that the attitude of the recruiter (or in our case the search committee chair, department chair, dean, etc.) affects the applicant's reaction to the institution and his or her intention to accept the position.

One would think that institutions of higher education would take the hiring process more seriously, if for no other reason than the fact that it represents a substantial commitment of time and expense to the institution. Direct costs (excluding the costs of faculty and staff time for those who serve on the search committee or interview the candidate and the lost operating costs associated with the unfilled position) for a presidential search can exceed $60,000 if a search firm is not used. When a search firm is used, an option more and more institutions are choosing for the recruiting of presidents and other senior officers, we need to add to the $60,000 figure 33 percent of the incumbent's first year's salary (assuming the salary is $125,000, this would represent an additional cost of $42,000) plus expenses ($10,000) for a total cost of $112,000 and up. This can be quite an expense since the latest studies indicate that the average length of term for a college president is now under five years.

The cost of hiring in other areas can be even more dramatic. In order to compete in the marketplace for faculty in the sciences, a dean must be prepared to put together a package that includes equipment, materials and supplies, graduate student and/or post-doctoral student support, secretarial support, summer support for the candidate, and moving expenses. In 1988–89, of the six faculty members hired at the State University of New York at Buffalo (UB) in the Faculty of Natural Sciences and Mathematics, the average start-up cost amounted to $127,333 each (from a low in mathematics of $6,000 to a high of $214,000 in physics and astronomy). In 1989–90, eight faculty members were hired at an average start-up cost of $130,375 (from a low of $20,000 in mathematics to a high of $241,000 in physics and astronomy).

It turns out that at UB it did not make a substantial difference if a full professor or an assistant professor was hired. While the highest start-up cost of $241,000 was for a full professor in physics and astronomy, the next three highest costs ($200,000, $162,000, and $157,000) were for assistant professors in chemistry and biology.

Therefore, it seems reasonable to conclude that the substantial costs involved in hiring alone should convince the institutions that it is in their self-interest to do a better job of hiring than they are currently doing.

Such an effort may also pay handsome benefits in enhancing the retention rate of young faculty hires. Studies (Matier 1990, Smart 1990) have shown that faculty turnover is greatest at the assistant professor level. These studies have also found that faculty retention is enhanced where campus administrators are successful in "selecting new faculty whose professional orientations are consistent with institutional goals and activities" (Smart, p. 420).

But the attitude of individuals and the cost of a search are not the only factors that have an impact on the hiring process. The attitude of the committee or department as a body, as well as the candidate's own attitude, also affects the process. Hiring, especially at the senior faculty rank, is seen as a type of mating game and is approached with as much enthusiasm as a trip to the dentist.

The anecdotal experience reported by Rosovsky (1990) is illustrative, humorous, and all too true:

The deans have been ushered out, remnants of the lunch are gone. My next engagement is a wooing session: the groom is the Faculty of Arts and Sciences, represented by me, and the bride is a young philosopher teaching at a Midwestern university. My assignment is to convince him to accept a full professorship at Harvard University. It is an important assignment—nothing that I will do today matters more. Whenever an opportunity exists to raise average quality, a dean's heart beats faster, and all sorts of evidence indicate that this young man borders on genius. (The bride is very beautiful!) But that is not all. Our Philosophy Department is excellent, frequently ranked first in the country. The department is so good that it exhibits a classic pathology: the inability to find anyone worthy of joining its ranks. It is in imminent danger of becoming a club of old gentlemen, more exclusive with every retirement and death. In my imagination I picture the department with only one member: a patriarch holding a gigantic bag of black balls in his hand. And now, at last, a candidate!

For these reasons I determine to be as charming and persuasive as possible, and to make an extremely generous offer. With a smile on my face—attempting not to think of Pagliacci—I step into the reception area to greet my visitors, the young philosopher and his wife. These days her presence is not unusual. She is a computer programmer, and her views concerning Harvard and her own employment opportunities may determine the outcome of our courtship.

In my large and beautiful office I have done my best to create the right atmosphere. The fireplace is lit. Bottles of sherry and brandy are at hand (I am convinced that these amenities are less customary west of the Allegheny Mountains). Outside, it is raining and I note that the young philosopher has carelessly put his muddy shoes on the cushions of my new white couch. My administrative assistant will not be pleased.

We begin with the usual recruitment speech. Harvard is special, perhaps unique. It is a place where scholars can grow, offering the finest colleagues and students. I have never regretted moving to Harvard and neither will you. The Boston area is exciting, etc.[*] This is not, let me stress, a cynical speech. Most of it I deeply believe, although I realize that dozens of recruiters are saying similar things at other universities, with equal conviction. I can also

[*See H. Rosovsky, *The University: An Owner's Manual* (New York: W. W. Norton and Company, 1990), p. 49—eds.]

tell—and this is no surprise—that my visitors are not unfamiliar with this genre of exhortation. In all fields there is intense competition for the services of the finest scholars. Another offer is a familiar event. (The groom is anxious.)

The next part of the interview is also depressingly familiar. I have to listen to a recitation of everything that is wrong with Harvard, Boston, Cambridge, our departments, salaries, and so on. Housing is too expensive; public schooling is bad and private education is too expensive; the spouse sees few job opportunities; the Philosophy Department is much too small; good graduate students are going to Princeton; there is little collegiality at Harvard; *und so weiter.* There is some truth in all of these assertions, and their detailed and loving presentation is part of the bargaining game. (The bride is careful not to show too much enthusiasm.)

Soon we are dealing in specifics. I offer a high salary, inwardly cringing at equity considerations; add a most generous housing subsidy; throw in a small "slush fund"—sort of academic mad money; promise to help the spouse find a job and to get their one child into Cambridge's leading private school. Institutional generosity is greeted with expressionless faces. No words of gratitude. Instead, a new series of questions concerning sabbaticals, leaves, and retirement.

The hour is up. Others are waiting outside. An official offer letter will now have to be drafted, putting all my commitments on paper. I bid my visitors adieu and hand them over to the chairman of the Philosophy Department. For them a round of cocktail parties, dinners, a brief interview with President Bok, and time with real estate agents. For me, the *Harvard Crimson.* (pp. 48–50)

Hiring good candidates, like anything else, is an art, a combination of hard work and knowing what you're doing. Yes, sometimes it is luck; but luck has been defined as "when preparation meets opportunity."

The purpose of this book, then, is twofold. One, to identify and explain the roles played by key actors in the process of hiring. Two, to direct attention to special concerns and to provide guidelines and insights to the actors in carrying out the operation.

We look at a wide spectrum of issues related to the hiring process in universities and other higher education institutions. What makes our book particularly interesting and quite different is that it looks to those who have been successful in higher education for practical wisdom on the lessons they have learned and the information they wish to share.

In the early chapters we delineate the roles of the search committee, and of officials such as the president and the deans, in staffing a college or university. We look at what they must do to be effective hirers in this very competitive environment we now face. The focus then shifts to the candidate being hired and includes issues such as the hiring of star faculty and special targeted groups such as minorities and women along with guidelines to enhance recruitment initiatives.

A unique feature of this volume is that it includes a new dimension, one that is often ignored in mainstream discourse: the intersection of work and family. That is, problems involved in the hiring of dual-career couples are highlighted and the dilemmas that institutions face when they hire dual-career partners without consideration of their needs are dealt with.

As stated earlier, the costs of hiring are often phenomenal. And there are several dimensions, depending upon the institution, the position, and the candidate. Finally, we direct attention to lessons that can be gleaned from the private sector. We examine the advantages and disadvantages of using consultants and the role they should or should not play in the hiring process.

The need to be better informed is becoming increasingly acute. A number of converging factors have led to warnings that we will be facing a critical shortage of qualified administrators and faculty for our institutions of higher education over the next twenty years. It has been estimated that from 1990 to 2010 about 563,000 new faculty will need to be hired against a base of 663,000 current total faculty (Bowen and Schuster 1986).

We are beginning to see the popular press report on a number of studies that identify a critical faculty shortage in our institutions of higher education between now and the year 2010. These shortages result from the fact that as the baby boomers of World War II entered our institutions of higher education in the middle to late sixties, the institutions responded by rapidly increasing the faculty ranks. It was not unusual for institutions to literally add hundreds of new faculty members in a single year. The faculty who joined the academy in the mid-sixties are now nearing retirement age. Within five to seven years some of our departments will see their faculty retiring at rates of 25 percent or greater. For example, the president of Columbia University reports that nearly one-half of his tenured professors in the Arts and Sciences will retire in the 1990s. Nationally, it is estimated that from 1992 to the year 2012 about 153,000 new arts and sciences faculty will need to be appointed, which almost equals the number (156,000) of arts and sciences faculty currently at all four-year institutions (Bowen and Sosa 1989).

Between 1991 and 2005 the University of California system's nine campuses estimate that they will need to hire 10,200 faculty, 70 percent to replace retiring faculty and 30 percent for growth. It is estimated that at San Francisco State University 83 percent of tenure-track faculty will retire between the years 1983 and 2003 (El-Khawas, Cartwright, Fryer, Corrigan, and Marchese 1990).

Financial crises only seem to exacerbate the problem. Since wages and benefits can represent up to 85 percent of an institution's costs, one of the quickest and least traumatic ways of reducing these costs is through an early retirement plan. The construct of such a plan would be along the lines of offering the employees a bonus incentive if they retire by a fixed date. For example, in 1991 the City College of New York offered their eligible faculty and staff an early retirement option. Those individuals of at least fifty-five years of age and who had worked twenty-three years could receive 45 percent of their current salary contributed as a lump sum payment to their retirement plan. It was projected that five hundred people would take the early retirement option. Imagine their surprise when 980 retired early. While budgetary restrictions required that a number of these positions remain unfilled, the number of new faculty to be hired far exceeded anyone's expectations.

As for the students who were the cause of the faculty increase in the mid- to late sixties, they were similarly encouraged by the tremendous expansion to go on and complete Ph.D. programs. However, when they completed their Ph.D. programs in the early seventies, the job market had already become saturated, the economy had turned bad, and there were no jobs for these newly minted faculty. Consequently, Ph.D. programs saw dramatic reductions in the number of individuals who chose college teaching as a career. The increase in the number of faculty approaching retirement age and the decrease in the number of doctoral candidates have caused forecasters to make dire predictions about the available pool of replacement college faculty in the years to come. Bowen and Sosa are often quoted as predicting that by 1997 arts and sciences departments will find only seven people applying for every ten faculty vacancies.

The picture is no brighter for faculty in the sciences and engineering. Atkinson (1989) reports that, barring substantial government intervention, as we enter the next century our universities will produce seventy-five hundred fewer science and engineering Ph.D.s each year than are needed to meet the demands of the nation. Even this number is deceptive owing to the dramatic increase in the number of foreign nationals enrolled in these doctoral programs. In the physical sciences, U.S. doctorate recipients decreased from 82.2 percent in 1970 to 62.5 percent in 1986; in engineering, the drop was from 73.2 percent to 40.8 percent (Association of American Universities 1989, p. 3). While the presence of the brightest foreign students in our Ph.D. programs provides a certain richness, the potential for increased shortages exists when countries like China and Korea suddenly encourage their students to return home, appealing to their desire to support their nation's new initiatives in science and technology transfer.

In addition, it should come as no surprise that non-Asian minorities and women continue to be underrepresented in the faculty pool. As recently as 1987 less than 1 percent of the physical science and engineering Ph.D.s awarded to U.S. citizens was earned by blacks and only 6.59 percent of the engineering Ph.D.s went to women.

Adding to the problem of a faculty shortage are the surprising indications that we are experiencing a mini baby boom in this country. In 1990 the number of registered births was the highest since 1961 (National Center for Health Statistics, personal communication, June 1990). Of this number, 40 percent were firstborn. We already know that high school enrollments that have fallen from 1976 to a low of 12 million in 1990 are projected to climb to 17.8 million by year 2000 ("Projections," 1990). It now appears that this growth vector is continuing and perhaps even accelerating. If this trend is true, it will mean that the college-age cohort will increase through the early years of the next century, placing an additional demand on the supply of new faculty over and above the need for replacement faculty.

A number of other factors also enter into the equation. During the last twenty years we have witnessed increased competitiveness among colleges as more and more strive to enter the top ranks of their class. Excellence becomes the buzzword for institutions of higher education as those at the very top are rewarded with increased federal grants, state funds, prestige, gifts to their foundations, student applicants, etc. Therefore, there is a heightened sense of a need to hire "stars." This translates into institutions engaging in recruiting wars and faculty members being willing to go to the highest bidder.

Finally, there is competition between higher education and the nonacademic markets, especially in the high technology areas. The increased demands on American industries to compete in the world economies, especially by Japan and Western European countries, have caused American campuses to greatly increase their own investments in science and technology. We find more and more Ph.D.s in engineering and science being recruited away from our colleges by lucrative offers from the industrial sector. It is likely that other changes, like the move to a European community and the Free Trade Agreements with Canada and Mexico, will only exacerbate this problem in years to come.

Ironically, as we face this critical shortage of individuals available to teach and lead our institutions of higher education into the twenty-first century, these same institutions have never been more poorly prepared to meet the challenge of hiring. It is this gap that, through this book, we are aiming to fill. Our intention is to look at the art of hiring from a number of dimensions and, thereby, guide those in the hiring business on how best to perform the art of hiring.

We are excited about this book, for in many ways it is the first of its kind in American higher education. And yet, it addresses a problem that all of us in the academy so dearly feel.

REFERENCES

American Association of Universities. 1989. *The Federal Role in Doctoral Education* [Policy statement]. Washington, D.C.: Author.

Atkinson, R. C. 1989. "Supply and Demand for Science and Engineering Ph.D.s: A National Crisis in the Making." Remarks to the Regents of the University of California, February 16, 1989.

Bowen, H. R., and J. H. Schuster. 1986. *American Professors: A National Resource Imperiled.* New York: Oxford University Press.

Bowen, W. G., and J. A. Sosa. 1989. *Prospects for Faculty in the Arts and Sciences: A Study of Factors Affecting Demand and Supply, 1987 to 2012.* Princeton, N.J.: Princeton University Press.

El-Khawas, E., C. Cartwright, T. W. Fryer, R. Corrigan, and T. Marchese. 1990. "Faculty Shortages: Will Our Responses Be Adequate?" [Excerpt from session at 1990 American Association for Higher Education National Conference]. *American Association for Higher Education Bulletin* 42 (10): 3–7.

Harris, M. M., and L. S. Frank. 1987. "A Field Study of Applicant Reactions to Employment Opportunities: Does the Recruiter Make a Difference?" *Personnel Psychology* 40: 765–84.

Hynes, W. J. 1990. "Successful Proactive Recruiting Strategies: Quest for the Best." In *Enhancing Departmental Leadership,* J. B. Bennett and D. J. Figuli, eds. New York: American Council on Education/Macmillan, pp. 51–60.

Matier, M. W. 1990. "Retaining Faculty: A Tale of Two Campuses." *Research in Higher Education* 31 (1): 39–60.

Rosovsky, H. 1990. *The University: An Owner's Manual.* New York: W. W. Norton and Company.

Prospects for Faculty in the Arts and Sciences. 1989. Princeton, N.J.: Princeton University Press.

Smart, J. C. 1990. "A Causal Model of Faculty Turnover Intentions." *Research in Higher Education* 31 (5): 405–23.

2

The Role of the President
in the Hiring Process

Joseph F. Kauffman

There is a substantial body of descriptive and analytical literature
on the college and university presidency. It is not possible here to
delineate the various roles a president* plays or the conflicting expectations of the president that different constituent groups within
the university hold. Yet it seems clear that a president is the one
person who must view the institution as a whole while others may
be vigorous advocates for the part of the institution for which they
are responsible. The president, therefore, is concerned with balancing
interests, with priorities, perceptions of quality, morale, anticipating
and preventing dysfunctional conflicts and similar matters, along with
the traditional outcome goals of colleges and universities. The external environment in which the institution operates must also be
a consideration, even though it may not be subject to a president's
control. Above all, the president can and should have considerable

---

*The term "president" is used throughout, although in many public institutions
the campus head may have the title of chancellor.

influence in setting a tone for campus values, expectations, and standards.

In many ways, the president is the steward of the institution's integrity—its guardian. Although others have serious responsibilities, it is the president who approves or disapproves the recommendations that result from the deliberations of others. In addition, appointments and those policy matters that must have governing board approval are accompanied by the recommendation of the president. One of the concerns raised about the relatively brief terms of presidential service in recent years relates to this guardian role. If a president is not concerned with the institution as a whole, and its future, the long-term outlook for that institution is seen as placed in jeopardy. A succession of short-term presidencies precludes such a long-term outlook. How to institutionalize an ongoing concern with quality and integrity is a crucial challenge and governing boards look to their presidents for the answer.

STAFFING A COLLEGE OR UNIVERSITY

One can develop a variety of lists of key functions of administration or of a president's responsibilities. Along with leadership, representation, and financial concerns would certainly be the topic of staffing an institution. Staffing includes the hiring and retention of excellent, productive faculty, administrators, and support service personnel. Obviously, the president does not achieve all of this personally. To a considerable extent, the hiring process is institutionalized, with delegated responsibilities to deans, departments, and other units. But it is the president who is ultimately responsible for approving or disapproving a search committee's effort. It is the president who sets the expectations, participates as needed, sees to it that institution-wide policies about equity and affirmative action are implemented, accurate information is provided to candidates, and, finally, that new staff is properly welcomed and oriented. All of this can be, and sometimes is, routinized, but a vigilant president can never take for granted that staffing needs little of one's attention. A college or university is its faculty and staff. The work of that faculty and staff is what students experience.

What follows is, of necessity, a general statement concerning the role of the president and the various considerations involved in the hiring process. While all of this will apply to all presidents, the specific manner in which presidents inject themselves directly into the process will differ according to institutional distinctiveness, size, mission, and role. Certainly the day-to-day involvements of a president of a major public research university will differ from that of a president of a small, church-related college. The reader can imagine other illustrations as well.

The whole subject of hiring college and university presidents is separate from what follows. I have written on that subject and conducted presidential searches as well. Readers will find a substantial body of writing on presidential hiring. This chapter presumes that a president is in place and speaks to the responsibilities of that president in the hiring of faculty and administrators.

There was a time when presidents hired the faculty and everyone else employed by a college. The founding presidents of colleges and early presidents of eighteenth- and nineteenth-century colleges did just that. Institutional histories of places such as the Johns Hopkins University tell of the founding president putting together the small number of initial faculty. I was involved in the early beginnings of Brandeis University and observed directly the responsibility taken by its founding president, Abram L. Sachar, for the hiring of faculty and staff. His continuing involvement, after the hiring of the first dozen faculty members, was not always appreciated. When the University of Wisconsin created two new institutions in 1966, University of Wisconsin-Green Bay and University of Wisconsin-Parkside, the president selected a chancellor for each and those two chancellors went about hiring the initial faculty and staff. All of this represents an extremely rare opportunity. Institutions cannot start all over again, and all but a rare few presidents inherit almost their entire faculty and staff—even those top staff from within the institution who competed against them for the presidential position. Usually, a majority of the full-time faculty will be tenured and administrative staff will have various rights related to their seniority. With skillful and sensitive preparation, a president may be able to reshape the top management team over a period of two to three years. It is not without consequences, however. With the hiring of faculty, it will be business as usual unless a new president signals an interest and determination to get involved.

Today, except for positions in the president's own cabinet or office, the president's direct involvement is usually in meeting prospects or candidates that others, departments or deans, are trying to recruit to consider vacant positions. Such meetings are less for screening purposes and more for aid in convincing a person to move from one institution to another. Institutions have images and reputations regarding their work environment, availability of physical facilities, financial future, and similar matters. The president reinforces or counters such images and reputations, if they are questionable, and provides assurances about future directions. The president can answer questions authoritatively. For the most promising prospective faculty such assurances may have to do with research space and funding, computing assistance, research support, and the like. For prospective senior administrative staff, an interest in the longevity of the current president, reporting relationships, unit budgets, and such concerns will be paramount. The president, and especially the attitude and morale of the president, will tend to attract or discourage those being recruited to be either a serious candidate or to actually accept an offer of an appointment. A president's time invested in such activities is well spent.

WHEN A VACANCY OCCURS

As the chief executive officer of an institution, the president is responsible for the wise use of precious resources. The most significant expenditures of an institution are for personnel, and there is constant pressure to add staff and faculty positions. This is especially so for administrative support staff as litigation, auditing, compliance reporting, and student support programs have expanded. While there may be valid reasons for the growth of administrative staff, the faculty, trustees, and legislators will look to cuts in this category as reductions of staff have to be made. In the March 28, 1990 issue of the *Chronicle of Higher Education*, Karen Grassmuck reported that, nationally, support staff positions (nonfaculty) grew in number more than 60 percent between 1975 and 1985. During this same decade the number of faculty increased less than 6 percent. In these difficult economic times there will definitely be some reductions and reallocation of funds and positions.

Each position represents an expenditure of resources to perform tasks that are central to the institution's mission and purpose. Just as the president makes a case for creating new positions, justifying the need for the use of such resources, positions that become vacant require a similar justification before authorizing them to be filled. In the area of administration, vacancies represent an opportunity to revisit administrative organization, workloads, and institutional priorities. Do we want to retain the same job description and reporting lines? Do colleagues have suggestions for improving or making more effective an operation now that there is an opportunity to make changes? If a particular post has had a succession of short-term or unsuccessful incumbents, is there something wrong with the way that position is structured? Colleges and universities reallocate resources all the time as a way of meeting changing needs, addressing changing priorities, or coping with budget reductions. Redesigning an administrative organization is a part of this process and staff vacancies represent a unique opportunity to review staffing before authorizing the filling of a vacancy. I am not necessarily suggesting a total reduction of staff but, instead, the president's opportunity to redeploy staff positions in the most rational manner in a changing institutional climate. Vacancies represent opportunities to reexamine institutional needs and presidents should insist on such reexamination.

On the academic side, faculty position vacancies should also be regarded as a chance to reexamine program direction, respond to new needs, strengthen programs that one's institution is committed to, and make teaching loads more equitable. We tend to do this with physical space resources more than we do with faculty positions. Reallocating positions is the one tool presidents have to make some difference in an institution.

THE CHANGING ENVIRONMENT

When a faculty position is authorized to be filled, academic department personnel committees, typically, advertise the position vacancy and bring it to the attention of graduate departments offering the doctoral degree in that academic field. Institutional policies on affirmative action will be complied with and a final choice will be recommended by the department to the school or college dean. The president is usually shielded from any involvement, other than the pro forma approval of the outcome. But there are all sorts of new considerations today that make the typical and routine of yesterday questionable. These result from the changing environment in which our institutions exist. These considerations include, among others, the changing demographics of our country, including not only racial and ethnic factors but the great need to accommodate women's needs in our institutions. They also include new market factors affecting both compensation and morale. The litigious atmosphere in which we operate is still another factor that affects the hiring process. All of these raise questions that require the direct involvement and concern of the president.

Demographic

Readers are familiar with the demographic facts and figures. The characteristics of the population of the United States are changing rapidly. In the next decade a significant proportion of those entering the labor force will be Hispanics, Blacks, and Asians. The elementary and secondary schools of most cities are already experiencing these changes and colleges and universities will be expected to adapt successfully. For the most part, our faculties are predominantly white and male. We are urged to take steps to hire more Hispanic, Black, and Asian faculty and staff. There are shortages of Black and Hispanic Ph.D.s and graduate students, especially in the academic fields where positions are needing to be filled. Pressures to increase minority faculty and staff hiring will grow and, often, will be accompanied by tensions and conflict.

Success in meeting this challenge is most often related to the commitment and involvement of the president. Making positions and funds available, insisting on extra effort in recruiting minorities, stressing the importance of the diversity of faculty, as well as students, to the quality and credibility of the educational experience—all of these flow from the president's leadership. Attracting minority faculty and staff to a campus requires the further step of achieving a campus climate that is seen as hospitable and attractive. Here, too, the president is a vital force in shaping a climate for diversity. The grapevine conveys the word that an institution and its leaders are serious about building such a climate or, conversely, that it is not a good place to live and work.

Women constitute a majority of college students today and will constitute a majority of those persons joining the labor force in the next decade. Women are no longer confined to the so-called feminine occupations and our institutions are adjusting to a whole new set of realities related to their employment. A university's office of human resources must now grapple with issues of spousal hiring, flex-time, extension of tenure review, child care, family sick-care days, and similar matters.

It used to be that a department recruiting a distinguished or promising scholar might, occasionally, have to offer to assist in finding a suitable job in the community for that person's wife. In recruiting outstanding women and men today, the need also to hire the spouse is much more common. Hiring policies must deal with this new factor. The willingness to fill posts with spouses of new hires usually conflicts with an institution's affirmative action guidelines. Increasingly, married women cannot be attracted to accept a new position unless their husbands, also academics, are given an appropriate appointment as well. Presidents need to involve faculty governance bodies in finding a solution to this problem. It will not be easy.

The old idea that equity required that everyone be treated the same precluded flexible work schedules for women, based on the ages of their children. Industry has dealt with this problem for many years and colleges and universities are learning to adapt to this as well. In some cases, two-person jobs are created, although the issue of fringe benefits can be a problem. For faculty positions, women with very young children may make a case for an extension of time for tenure review. The hiring policies should be clear as to what exceptions are possible and the process for seeking exceptions.

One sure way to recruit and hire excellent women staff is to provide adequate child-care facilities and services. These may be subsidized or completely self-supporting. The availability of such services seems to be a major item in the consideration of where to seek employment. A personnel policy that communicates to women an understanding of family-care needs that are recognized as legitimate will go a long way in making an institution an attractive employer. Presidents must see to it that these issues are faced creatively and responsibly.

Market Factors

Market factors have an impact on the hiring process and presidents must deal not only with an inadequate pool of potential faculty in some fields but with new challenges to compensation policy, salary compression, and the morale problems that flow from all of this. We are all aware of the fact that a majority of the Ph.D. students in many fields of engineering, computer science, and mathematics are from foreign countries. Complaints about the English proficiency of teaching assistants in these fields are common. Presidents have learned that average faculty salaries will not attract qualified faculty in engineering, computer science, finance, accounting, and other fields for which private sector employment is an alternative. We have adjusted to this reality in medicine and law but market forces have affected many other academic fields beyond these professional schools. A recent survey of salaries of college and university administrators, reported in the January 23, 1991 *Chronicle of Higher Education,* reveals that the salaries of deans of dentistry, medicine, veterinary medicine, and law schools are significantly higher than those of presidents.

The emerging picture is that there is a scarcity of persons for such teaching fields and, often, salary offers must be higher than the average salaries paid to other faculty. Further, veteran faculty members at the associate or full professor levels are resentful at having new, younger faculty joining their departments at salaries equal to or higher than their own salaries. The salary compression that results from this situation shatters bonds of institutional loyalty and signals that one may have to leave, or threaten to leave, in order to receive a market-level salary. Those institutions where faculty collective bargaining is a factor have experienced bruising conflicts over salary and incremental differences resulting from these market forces. It is true that Humanities faculty positions can be filled at lower salaries than Business faculty positions, but that does not always result in it being seen as an acceptable practice for an institution. A union philosophy of across-the-board raises also runs counter to these same market forces.

Presidents must not only be aware of these changes but must develop strategies and policies for dealing with them. The morale of a faculty is a crucial ingredient in the educational environment. Prospective faculty tune in quickly to faculty morale and faculty resentments, and their employment decisions are influenced greatly by their perceptions.

There are a number of other issues tied to compensation and they need to be reviewed. Some institutions have a policy of hiring replacement faculty at the lowest rank and extending the periods for promotion as long as possible. Other institutions try to hire faculty at the upper ranks, relying on recruitment of successful faculty from other institutions. In the decade ahead there will be shortages of faculty in a number of academic disciplines and these policies need presidential and governing board review. An institution requiring an extended period in rank before eligibility for promotion will both discourage gifted aspirants and be vulnerable to aggressive recruiting efforts by competing institutions.

The question of initial salaries, set upon appointment, is directly related to the hiring process. A market mind-set would conclude that you pay what you have to pay to hire someone. In some fields, starting salaries have to be quite high. In others, however, there is a considerable amount of discretion. It may be possible to obtain two assistant professors for one retiring professor. That may be attractive in some cases but it may overlook needed program strengthening that is important for the long term. In public universities these days, it is impossible to assure anyone of future salary increments. Frequently, legislative appropriation bills mandate the amount or percentage of such increments. Sometimes the actual record of the past few years is discouraging to prospective faculty appointees. My one view is that it is wise to use the considerable discretion that usually exists in setting the starting salary. Since you cannot assure anyone of the size of future compensation increases, the highest justifiable starting salary offer becomes the only leverage you have. If every unit is doing its own thing on these matters, the institution's overall interests and future are not well served. A president must be in control of compensation and rank policies and an overall strategy must be in effect.

HIRING ADMINISTRATORS

The hiring of administrators is usually different from the hiring process for faculty. For the most part, campuswide search committees are appointed by the president or a designee, comprised of constituent representatives and staff from the administrative unit involved. Often, the search committee membership is not experienced in the professional field under consideration, but political factors may require such representation. Thus, positions such as Registrar, Director of Admissions, Business Manager, Library Director, and the like are often the focus of large search committees with little experience. In recent years the filling of a major administrative post has often become contentious in ways never before imagined. Should there be representatives of all constituent groups on the committee? Should students be included? Should they all have an opportunity to interview candidates? Should there be a purposeful balancing of men and women, minority and others, and on and on? In some institutions, union and nonunion representation may be an issue. The process itself may become more of an issue than the goal of the effort—to search and screen for candidates for a particular position. Participation by relevant individuals can be important and searches do need legitimation, but in many cases there is excessive participation. Participation is not an end in itself. It should be functional in order to be valid.

Presidents should review the policies and procedures of administrator searches. Do they all require search committees? Are search committees too large or, in some cases, dysfunctional? Hiring implies that the best possible pool of prospects and candidates has been developed and screened, out of which a very few can be recommended to the appointing authority. Unfortunately, in the amateur way in which most searches are conducted, a significantly large pool of candidates has not been unearthed. Rather, a perfunctory vacancy notice has been advertised and most of the search committee's energy has been spent on screening the limited number of persons who apply in response to such a notice. Recruiting prospects for consideration is the most difficult and important task of a search. Without an adequate pool of prospects, the search will not succeed.

A special note needs to be made here concerning public institutions and the spread of state legislation requiring open records for personnel searches. The mass media have been effective in convincing lawmakers that confidentiality equals secrecy and the public's right to know must be the first priority. There are an increasing number of states with requirements that searches be conducted in the open.

The press may have access to the names, résumés, and letters of recommendation of all candidates, or at least the finalists. In some states, interviews with candidates must be open to the press. While the press pays attention primarily to presidential searches, it can also reveal information for others as well. Developing an adequate pool of prospects or candidates becomes very difficult under these circumstances. If each person nominated must be told that his or her candidacy will be known to the press, many successful and secure administrators will decline to be considered. That is certainly true of my own experience with presidential searches. Some institutions have resorted to the use of executive search firms and consultants in an effort to reduce the consequences of such requirements. But it is a continuing, if not growing, problem that will challenge the hiring process.

Presidents must also be involved in seeing to it that a proper charge is delivered to a search committee. Who will describe the nature of the appointment, the description of the duties of the position, the qualities and experience needed by the person to fill the post? Who will do the background checking and the interviewing? What will the budget for the search be? Will the committee bring forth several unranked names or merely recommend one? Assuming the president or his or her designee is the appointing authority, such questions should all be answered in advance and stated in the charge to the committee.

Finally, on the conduct of searches, the president must be prepared to reject all of the finalists if no one is satisfactory. While the president is bound to select from the list formulated by the appointed search committee, the president is never freed from the responsibility of appointing someone for whom the president alone is accountable. "I didn't really have confidence in this person but the committee recommended him" is not a defensible posture of the president. Governing boards approve personnel appointments upon the recommendation of the president. While sending a search committee back to the task, or reopening a search, is not pleasant, it may be necessary from time to time. Further, it may send an important message to a campus concerning the standards and high expectations of a president.

IMPACT OF LITIGATION

I mentioned the litigious atmosphere earlier when discussing the changing environment in which colleges and universities operate today. I mean by this the fact that the courts have increasingly granted judicial review of college and university actions to an extent never imagined when I first entered college administration in 1952. This is especially true in public institutions, although independent institutions have been affected as well. From complaints of unlawful discrimination in the hiring process to the implied obligations of a letter of appointment, one must be mindful of a need to make a record and to defend one's actions—in court, if necessary. This affects both the content and the style of communication in correspondence, interview, and in offers of employment. Such concerns may require some training and orientation for department heads and others who are involved in screening and hiring personnel. It will certainly require the input of legal counsel in the formulation of the contents of letters of appointment. Record keeping related to searches becomes a requirement as well.

All of this influences the style of discourse and communication. Some letters of appointment, or offers of appointment, in public institutions sound like impersonal legal documents. In my own work, I have often accompanied such letters with a handwritten note of welcome to try to overcome the guarded and defensive language and tone of the formal offer with its terms and conditions. Sometimes a personal telephone call is appropriate as well.

INDUCTING NEW STAFF

I do not regard the hiring process as complete without some consideration of the welcoming and orientation of new faculty and staff. An effective office of human resources will be productive in providing housing and community information, including schools, housing, banks, and religious institutions. Ways should be found to welcome newcomers each year and newcomers should be helped to know each other. There was a time when the wives of faculty members formed clubs or associations that took responsibility for this kind of welcoming activity. Times have changed but such needs still exist and institutions should seek to address them creatively.

Some kind of orientation will also be appropriate for newly hired faculty and staff. This may be done by departments in large universities or on a campuswide basis in smaller institutions. Above all, the president should not only see to it that such activities occur, but should be a participant in both the welcoming and orientation process. They represent a rare opportunity to transmit values and expectations.

PROFESSIONAL DEVELOPMENT AND ASSESSMENT

Finally, on this point, I believe that a president should see to it that there are opportunities for the professional development of staff, and that performance reviews are conducted. For faculty, the traditional means for professional development consists of attending and participating in regional or national meetings of one's academic discipline. While travel money for such purposes may be scarce, such activities are of great value. Further, in-house faculty development programs can provide assistance to faculty in a range of activities from student assessment techniques to grant proposal writing. When an institution replaces retiring faculty with younger persons at the lower ranks, such an investment becomes a necessity.

With administrative staff, many colleges and universities overlook the need for in-house professional development. Again, attendance at professional meetings is traditional, but a great deal can be accomplished within the institution by creating seminars and workshops that foster an understanding of an institution's history, mission, and governance and to explore the key issues that require attention if the institution is to flourish. I have been conducting such a professional development seminar at the University of Wisconsin-Madison for the past five years and it is well received by the participants. Unlike some organizations, universities do not usually have career ladders for administrative staff or well-devised methods of advancement. Ways have to be found to reinforce their bonds to the institution and professional development programs have the potential to aid in this.

As for performance assessment, new faculty obtain an understanding of the basis for retention, promotion, and tenure from their departments, dean, and faculty handbooks. They know that there will be a form of peer evaluation incorporating some assessment of teaching, scholarly endeavors, and service. New administrative appointees, however, rarely perceive what will be the criteria or process for assessing their performance. Often, the only perception is a political one: identifying the persons with whom you have to get along. I believe that presidents should see to it that there is a rational, equitable review process for administrators aimed primarily at their development and performance. I contrast this with the summative, pass-fail manner of evaluation. The hiring process should conclude with a new appointee made aware of the nature of the performance-review process so that there will be no surprises afterwards.

OTHER MATTERS

One could go on with details about moving expenses, loans for housing in seeking to get people to relocate to high-cost-of-living areas of the country, the special situation of church-related colleges and universities, enlisting the support of one's governing board or system administration in providing adequate salary support for positions, and more. In a sense, all of the topics covered in this volume are a part of the president's responsibility. The president must see to it that others carry out their duties properly for it is only the president, ultimately, who serves at the pleasure of the board.

I have, purposefully, omitted any attempt to treat the special problems involved with athletics. In NCAA Division I institutions, the hiring and firing of athletic directors and football or basketball coaches requires its own volume. Presidents often complain about problems with their medical schools, but big-time athletics cause far more stress. Presidents lose jobs over such matters and the political clout of athletic boosters can be enormous. In no other area of a university's activities are there more pressures for the hiring or firing of specific individuals.

University hospitals also represent unique problems in hiring as well as financing. The inherent conflicts between administrators and medical staff pose special problems, as does the locus of decision-making.

Public institutions may be required to be a part of a state civil service or classified system, which means that a substantial body of employees will be considered state employees. Their job descriptions, classification, and salary levels may be determined by others, as will be rights to transfer, eligibility for jobs, and such matters. Further, there may be employee unions and agreements that preclude institutional prerogatives in several areas. All of this is to admit that there are many aspects of the hiring process that cannot be dealt with adequately in a general treatment of the subject. A president must become familiar with all of these aspects in order to be effective.

SUMMARY

In summary, many different people are responsible for, and participate in, the hiring process in our colleges and universities. The unique purposes of our institutions of higher learning require an organization that is less hierarchical than most businesses and government agencies. Our society depends upon our institutions' commitment to merit and excellence—to knowing the difference between quality and the absence of quality and having the courage to act on that difference. Men and women who strive for excellence want to be in an environment that recognizes and rewards outstanding achievements. It is for this reason that the hiring process becomes so crucial in signaling to everyone the true values and standards of an institution.

The president must insist on high expectations, consonant with the mission of a particular institution. The president's own office and staff should be a model for others. If the president tolerates inadequacy in his or her top appointees, it is difficult to preach a different message to others. For a time, a man or woman is privileged to serve as the president of a college or university. That service, however long, should leave the institution better than it was in terms of the faculty and staff hired. That is a sufficient measure of a president's accomplishment.

3

The Role of the Dean
in the Hiring Process

Donald W. Jugenheimer

Administrators, faculty, students, and governing boards each believe they run the university—or think they should. So to faculty, deans may seem to be superfluous to the process of screening and hiring new faculty, while deans may see themselves in a central role. In reality, the dean's place is somewhere between these two extremes.

Screening faculty candidates should ideally be the province of current faculty. Hiring, of course, involves administrative inputs, so the dean enters the process. Yet the dean should play an essential, although perhaps occasionally tangential, position throughout the new-faculty screening and hiring process.

Some deans may take on the entire task of hiring. They compose the job description. They place announcements and advertisements. They have all inquiries, nominations, applications, and supporting materials addressed to themselves. They carry out most of the interviewing process. They make the hiring choice. Then they handle the necessary appointment paperwork.

Most important, they are wrong.

When deans control the hiring process, myopia and even blindness enter in, and the result is too often a homogeneity in the faculty. When any one person hires, that person tends to hire in his or her own image. A homogeneous faculty is a weak faculty. The strength of a university, or of any unit within the university, is diversity gained from exchanges of views, specialties, backgrounds, experiences, goals, and perceptions. When a single person takes responsibility for hiring, the weakness of homogeneity results. When a dean screens and hires, this homogeneity inevitably creeps in, which is perhaps the best reason for full faculty involvement in the hiring process. The faculty already are convinced they should be responsible for search-and-screen operations, not least because they want to avoid hiring more persons in the image of deans.

Still, the dean plays an important and essential role, which takes place before, during, and after the hiring process. And this role involves more than simply handling the ever-present paperwork.

In considering the role of the dean in hiring, let us take the larger view and examine the situation from the perspective of the college (assuming the dean administers a college in a larger university) and institution, rather than only from the perspective of the dean.

TWO MAJOR RESPONSIBILITIES

If the dean does not screen and hire, what is the dean's responsibility in the faculty hiring process? Actually, there are two major responsibilities: budget and standards. Deans are always interested in the financial repercussions of any and all decisions, so the budgetary responsibility should be obvious. The accountability for standards may be somewhat more recondite.

STANDARDS

The dean has a primary responsibility for maintaining college and institutional standards. Of course, the faculty will maintain standards, too: maintaining standards cannot be a task that is assigned somewhere for someone else to worry about. Everybody in the hiring process must retain a concern for maintaining standards—including the candidates.

But there are times when the faculty view of maintaining standards differs from the institutional interests. Take the case of a department with a strong research faculty, most of whom teach mainly because they are forced to do so, most of whom prefer to concentrate on their research, and most of whom would prefer to "farm out" the teaching responsibilities to someone else—anyone else, for that matter. The faculty would especially like to rid themselves of the undergraduate introductory "survey" courses—the ones that frustrate senior faculty because of the "dumb" questions and problems with teaching those "slow" undergraduates in large sections at a lowest-common-denominator level with so many papers to grade. The faculty's solution: hire some young novice without much scholarly ambition and let that person teach those courses. Of course, not all of these strategies are spelled out in the prior requests or position descriptions: just some allusion to "strong teaching required."

Even the department chair may be in on this ploy. This strategy may also be to the department chair's advantage. Hiring someone only to teach contributes to the division of labor and faculty specializations. The chair might foresee fewer complaints from the department faculty, especially from senior faculty, about teaching assignments. Having a "teaching faculty" member would probably contribute to easier scheduling and coverage for the department's course offerings. Finally, freeing up the other faculty might provide for increased research productivity and grants activities by the other faculty, who are most interested in research and scholarship.

Even if the chair is not involved in this approach, the chair may be bullied or coerced by various faculty pressures to go along with the tactic. Here, the dean becomes the major person with responsibility for maintenance of standards. The dean looks ahead to the eventual tenure decision and makes certain that all those hired show promise of clearing that hurdle. Certainly teaching is an important part of a faculty member's assignments, but at most institutions a well-rounded approach is a surer path to tenure success.

Does this mean that nobody should ever be hired primarily for teaching? Of course not. But it does mean those hired for teaching should also meet the required standards for scholarship and service, or there should be an alternate track for tenure, or the persons with primary teaching responsibilities may be hired for a finite term—most often with the title of "lecturer"—instead of on tenure track.

But the faculty, and especially the chair, will resist hiring for a finite term. There is less assurance of retaining the position for the longer term that way. A tenure-track position is more likely to be a permanent position. Again, the dean must be aware of the standards, in this case both the standards for hiring and the need for budgetary flexibility.

Another case where faculty may not adhere to "standards" is when older professors, sometimes without terminal degrees, see a threat from "hot" new Ph.D.s and so steer the search process toward someone more like themselves. It should be obvious how this strategy might result in the lowering of faculty standards. Sometimes this tactic is seen in the form of arguments for experience in lieu of degrees, especially in professional disciplines where practical or external work experience is often an important consideration. The outcome may even be expressed by a search committee member ranking a less-qualified candidate higher than a fully-qualified person.

Again, the dean needs to monitor to maintain standards. If a terminal degree is an advantage, it should be stated in the job description and adhered to in the hiring process. If the dean suspects that a search committee is approaching its task more for personal goals than for college or institutional objectives, conferral or even confrontation may be required. The easy way out is to expect the best, assume that everyone is doing "the right thing," and overlook or ignore these kinds of situations. But the result is too often an erosion of standards, so the dean must take the "high road" and make certain that others follow the same path.

Standards are not as much of a problem when hiring faculty "stars" who are intended single-handedly to provide significant improvements to an entire specialty or discipline. Now the focus shifts to the support required to attract such a stellar individual, as well as a salary that is very likely to exceed the normal boundaries. The dean's task may also include promoting and selling the necessity of such a position to higher administrators, who usually are pressured from all directions and are thus included to distribute resources rather evenly instead of in a lump sum for one unit.

BUDGET

The dean's other major responsibility is the budget. A commitment to hire a faculty member is also a budgetary commitment. Resources are limited by nature, and budget resources are especially limited. Usually, acquiring a faculty position for one unit enjoins such a position for some other unit. Committing enough funds to afford a middle- or upper-level newcomer, or to afford an entirely new hire in an expensive field, may substitute for multiple positions that might be afforded elsewhere.

Bringing in someone with tenure brings with it even more commitments. If a tenured faculty member stays thirty years, and if fringe benefits average a third of salaries, and if salaries are increasing at a reasonable (5 percent) annual rate, the total commitment for a $30,000 hire amounts to two and two-thirds million dollars (and even more if summer teaching receives extra pay)!

These costs escalate rapidly if start-up costs are involved, such as for laboratory space and equipment, often in the sciences, as well as for moving costs and similar categories of expenses. Scientific laboratories may run into six figures, often dwarfing the direct salary expenses. A commitment to a particular line of research is usually involved as well, with that commitment running well into the future.

This huge total cost is one good reason for the dean to pay special attention when a faculty candidate asks for tenure "up front." It's a budget commitment for that person's lifetime, which will affect many deans to come. It may also upset current faculty, those on tenure track and those with tenure who feel (and rightfully so) that tenure is a collegial decision. So now we begin to understand why so many institutions no longer confer tenure on a newly hired person—and why any tenure decision should undergo the standard faculty review process.

At institutions that do confer tenure "up front," as it is known, it is still best if it is not conferred administratively. Any candidate who deserves immediate tenure should surely be able to clear a college and university review process. In the rare case when tenure is being considered to attract a young "hotshot" who has not had tenure at his or her previous institution, review by the standard faculty committees seems even more crucial.

These two responsibilities of the dean, standards and budget, arise throughout the faculty hiring process. Although there may be more facets of the dean's involvement during the hiring process, the critical phases may really come before and after the hiring.

BEFORE THE HIRING

Before there can be any hiring, a position must be reaffirmed and reauthorized. Even an existing position that is vacated must be authorized for it to be filled. The dean's task is to identify critical vacancies. That will not be difficult, because every department chairperson will gladly provide a list of vacancies, needs, desired specialties and special requirements, differences between this particular unit and its peers, and reasons to give priority to this program in preference to any others.

The dean's problem, then, is neither locating vacancies nor justifying that they be filled. Diplomacy, judgment, tact, persuasion, insight, and a reliable calculator will all be required, however. Deciding the priority order of all the requests is difficult, not least because any decision will please only a few while angering and disappointing many. The resulting decisions will impact on the standards of the college and the institution for years to come.

In upholding standards the dean must also review affirmative action procedures and make certain they are followed. It takes only one hiring cycle to learn that it is easier to remind the search committee *in advance* of affirmative action processes and purposes than it is to try to fix things after the fact. Good intentions are definitely not enough; good records and reasons are much better, legally, morally, and practically.

Budget considerations in advance of the hiring process parallel this concern for standards. Once vacancies have been identified and set in priority order, it is still necessary to "sell" one's recommendations to higher authorities. Everybody has needs, and every dean can justify every request. But there are more requests and more justifications than there are positions and funds. The problem is to gain funding and hiring authorization, especially without too many trade-offs and "deals."

Deals may be a way of life in campus politics, but they usually come back to haunt us. There is no such thing as a secret deal: somebody will find out, and the greater the necessity of keeping a deal secret, the greater the problems created when the deal becomes known. Deals are often oral agreements, and both parties remember the parts that favor them, contributing to confusion, disappointments, and ill will, perhaps leading to new deals.

Worse, deals are inherently unfair. If they weren't, there would be no need to strike a deal. Deals with one party lead to more deals with that same party. And deals with one party also lead to deals with other parties.

Maybe not every need for faculty hiring is met with proper funding and hiring authorization, no matter how good the supporting evidence. Yet although trying to operate in the open may seem naive to many, it is safer, quicker, less embarrassing, and much more honest than the alternative.

In general, deals should be discouraged. A clear "paper trail" should be encouraged. Complete but concise written records provide a means of tracking agreements and contribute to full communication and knowledge for all involved parties.

Whether there are deals or not, when budgets are "tight," vacancies must be ranked in priority order, as was noted under the discussion of standards. The only question is, when are budgets *not* tight? For the past twenty years, each year has brought a warning that next year's budget will be tighter than ever before, and for the most part, those predictions have been accurate. Colleges and administrators are now doing more with less than ever before. Tight budgets are a way of life, making allocations and priorities more important than ever before.

The dean faces a unique role when a faculty "pair" of husband and wife must be considered. If both candidates are in the same discipline, having two vacant positions is rare enough so that creating special opportunities will probably be required. Special attention must be given to be certain that *both* persons are actually productive, desirable, and promising scholars and teachers. If the two candidates are in differing disciplines, special political and negotiating skills will be needed to convince another college's dean that this would be a good "hire" for both units.

DURING THE HIRING

Maintenance of standards becomes an even more critical factor during the actual hiring process. A dean's decisions that may seem unimportant or even trivial can be magnified if problems arise.

THE SEARCH COMMITTEE

Take, for example, the appointment of a search committee. Often there are guidelines or bylaws that prescribe this process and its outcome. The easiest approach is to use the same faculty members over and over again. Another common approach is to rotate the appointments, selecting those who have not served lately. Both approaches are flawed: they ignore the specifics of each position, the strengths and weaknesses of individual faculty members, and the balance of ranks and specialties needed to conduct a fair and thorough individual search.

Search committee membership is critical and not to be determined hurriedly. Junior faculty should be represented. Perhaps students and alumni should, too. In professional disciplines, external practitioners may lend an important perspective. Even support staff should be considered: who knows more about a department chair's responsibilities than the departmental secretary?

If the search and screening committee is proposed by the faculty or by a committee, the dean usually must review and approve its composition. The easiest approach is to give approval: why make waves over such an unimportant item? But if the dean has qualms about the search committee membership, it may signal some political strategy or secret agenda on the part of one group or another. The dean must not abdicate responsibility to review the appointments thoroughly, ascertaining fairness, equitable representation, a variety of viewpoints, and a thorough knowledge of what the vacant position requires.

At the same time, the dean should establish the working schedule for the search process. If no deadline is set, search committee deliberations may take years, literally. If too short a working time is allowed, a fair and thorough search may be impossible. There is the ever-present danger of starting a search during the fall semester, knowing that there is plenty of time in which to work, yet not finishing the process until late spring; in the meantime, good candidates withdraw or go elsewhere. The corollary is conducting a quick search late in spring or during the summer, hoping for a fall hiring; fewer good candidates are available then, and the tight timing encourages a haphazard and sloppy search.

The best approach is to try to search slightly ahead of the busiest competitive period, so the best candidates are still available, and to confine the search to a limit of about two months or slightly longer, which should suffice for a thorough search while maintaining a vigorous effort.

MEETING WITH CANDIDATES

The dean should meet with the final candidates for every position. The problem is: who are the final candidates? One solution is to meet with all candidates, but in a large and complex college with several searches in progress that may result in dozens of interviews, most of them with persons who will not be recommended for their respective vacancies, and thus will probably never visit the campus again.

Meeting only with the finalists presents a different problem: the finalists must then be invited back to the campus, requiring more time and especially more travel money. The alternative, not meeting with candidates at all, is a poor choice because it leaves the dean out of the hiring "loop," prevents the dean from knowing new faculty before they are hired, abdicates the hiring responsibility to others, and contributes to an impression that the dean is aloof and distant.

Unfortunately, the first approach, meeting with all qualified candidates, works best. Occasionally the dean will see promise in a candidate that others overlook, or may uncover shortcomings that others have missed. There are also cases where a strong candidate is eliminated by the search committee, and the dean can then review the procedure, perhaps even meeting with the search committee, to make certain fair criteria have been applied.

Every candidate should be given the best treatment available—

not luxury hotels, gourmet meals, and first-class travel, but a friendly, professional, welcoming attitude. Every candidate should be made to feel that the position is desirable and that the institution is a good place for one's career. Even the unsuccessful candidates will help spread the word about the caliber and quality of the institution.

FAIR AND HONEST EVALUATIONS

It is the dean's responsibility, then, to ascertain that fair and honest evaluations have been provided, not just for the successful candidate, but for all candidates. To accomplish this goal, the dean may need to review the *vitae* of all applicants, make notes on meetings with those brought for interviews, and follow up with those recommended by the search committee. Another necessity is maintaining contact with the search committee, most often through its chairperson: by showing a deep and benevolent interest in the search process, the dean can help the search committee complete its task successfully and skillfully. Just knowing of the dean's interest can cause a committee to take its work more seriously and to feel appreciated, while simultaneously providing feedback and reassurance to the dean that the job is in good hands.

The search committee should maintain regular contact with all active candidates, and promptly notify those no longer under consideration. But the dean can help supplement this communication by making it known to visiting candidates that the door is open (or the telephone is available) for follow-up questions and reassurances. When search procedures take up many months, occasional contact with the leading candidate, or conversations with the chosen candidate while all the paperwork clears the necessary channels, can keep the best candidate interested and available.

CANDIDATES MUST MEET CRITERIA

It may be obvious that the dean must make sure the selected individual—or all those recommended on a priority list—possesses the stated qualifications for the position. That's why it is surprising that this step is so often overlooked. Certainly the search committee should have handled this chore, but for one's own reassurance, take a few minutes, dig the job description out of the files, and review the candidate's credentials for a close match. Better still is to ask the search committee to provide this information with its recommendation.

It may also seem obvious that new criteria should not be applied after the fact, but again, it happens. One relatively common occurrence, especially with candidates in professional fields, is to reject a nominee without a terminal degree even though the job description only noted that a doctorate was *preferred*. If a doctorate is required for tenure track, or if a doctorate will automatically have preference over lesser degrees, say so "up front" so that applicants *and the search committee* are well aware of these standards.

In the same way, it is unfair to demand that *all* criteria, both required and desired, be met by the finalist. If all criteria are to be required, make that decision in advance. Do not change standards during the process, or if you must, reopen the search or close it down and start over again. That is not only the fair way to do things: it will also prevent affirmative action problems.

THE HIRING BUDGET

During the hiring process, the dean's budgetary considerations are relatively simple. The dean must usually approve the offer that is made, even if the offer is presented by the department chair. The dean has a clearer picture of the entire college budget and may also have a better idea of the institutional budget, although the dean's first allegiance may well be to the college.

The dean understands the additional costs, above salary, of fringe benefits. There may be collateral expenses or commitments, such as moving expenses and research support. For hires on an academic-year basis, be sure to address the possibility (or requirement) of summer teaching. Make clear whether the appointment is tenure-track and whether it is for a finite term: do not leave any doubt or uncertainty on the part of any newly hired faculty member. The candidate's department needs full information, too, of course.

AFTER THE HIRING

Finally, the task is completed—or is it? Paperwork may seem to be the major chore that follows the hiring process. Although that may be true, the preparation of paperwork is perhaps more often the task of the dean's secretary: a dean may tire of signing his or her name dozens of times a day, but it is still easier than learning what obscure information must be inserted in the lines on all those preprinted forms. If a dean wants to help with paperwork, perhaps the best contribution would be to acquire all that obscure information needed for all those forms.

And, there is still a need to maintain standards, even though the hiring process *per se* has ended.

COUNSEL APPOINTEES

When new faculty are hired on tenure track, they need counseling as to what is required for tenure. It is not sufficient just to point to the faculty handbook or to refer vaguely to the triadic categories of teaching, research, and service. Several helpful things can be done.

- If scholarship is the most important criterion, tell the candidate.

- Provide copies of the promotion and tenure forms.

- Suggest that the candidate work toward some achievements in all the indicated categories.

- Show the record of a recently successful tenure candidate.

- Provide a calendar that indicates when a final tenure review must take place, along with opportunities for early review.

- Offer (or require) interim reviews of accomplishments as they apply to tenure categories and standards.

In all the printed materials dealing with promotion and tenure, technical information and directions may be provided. But someone needs to tell newly hired faculty the "real" criteria, not just those that are published. Does teaching really count as much as research and service? What kinds of service are recommended? Do textbooks count? Do presentations count? Does grant activity merit special recognition?

Faculty can gain this kind of information through the campus "grapevine," but it will be incomplete, untimely, biased, and often incorrect. Gaining this information from the dean may help the new faculty member to feel wanted and appreciated. Certainly this kind of contact also helps the dean, so that when retention reviews begin, there is more on which to judge than only what is contained in the personnel files.

A slightly different situation exists when the newly hired faculty member has already been tenured elsewhere: that individual should already know what is required, at least in general terms. Still, counsel is needed: each institution has its own idiosyncracies regarding requirements for tenure, especially regarding what areas are stressed; if the newly hired person has been given tenure "up front," the dean might suggest how best to meet obligations so as to avoid criticism from those new colleagues who may object to instant reviews and conferrals.

One unwritten duty of the dean is to monitor faculty work, to encourage and cajole. Make sure that appointees fulfill the college and institutional goals, as well as their own. Faculty have primary responsibility for their own careers, but deans can be of immense help. Faculty also have responsibility to their unit, college, and institution, and again the dean can be of help by providing periodic focus, encouragement, and review.

SUMMARY

Even though the dean may not be directly responsible for screening and selecting new faculty, the dean plays an integral role in the hiring and appointing processes. The dean's major responsibilities are to maintain standards and to monitor the budget. These two tasks appear throughout the faculty hiring process.

Before the hiring and to check standards, the dean must identify critical vacancies and must review and uphold the affirmative action procedures and standards. Relevant to budget, the dean must gain the necessary funding and hiring authorizations. In times of tight budgets it is also necessary to set priorities for faculty vacancies.

During the hiring process, most of the dean's responsibilities lie in the area of standards. The dean usually appoints or approves the search and screening process; this task includes setting the search schedule and deadlines, as well as determining or reviewing the search committee membership. The dean should meet with candidates, or at least with the prime prospect. The dean needs to ascertain that a fair and honest evaluation was provided for all candidates, not just for the chosen one. Finally, under the heading of standards, the dean must make certain that the selected individuals meet the stated criteria. In this consideration, it is unfair to hold candidates or search committees to new criteria after the fact. It is also unfair to demand that all criteria, both required and preferred, are met.

In the hiring process itself, the dean's major budgetary responsibility is to approve the final offer before it can be made to the leading candidate. The salary offer is obviously the most important factor, but moving expenses, research support, and similar costs may come into play, as well as the costs of fringe benefits and the impact on the college and institutional budget.

After the hiring process, there is, of course, paperwork, which may be considered the final stage of the budget review and approval process. As for standards, the dean should be sure that tenure-track appointees understand the requirements and deadlines. This should include a frank appraisal of the "real" criteria, not just as they appear in formal publications. To help faculty meet their own and institutional goals, deans may need to monitor faculty work and encourage their progress.

As in so many things, the dean is middle management, which means that the dean is caught between the upper administration and the faculty, trying to serve both groups while keeping the college on track, watching the budget, and hiring the best available faculty—the real strength of any university.

4

The Search Committee:
Prospecting for Go(l)d[1]

Milton Greenberg

. . . you shall seek all day ere you find them; and when you have
them, they are not worth the search.

Shakespeare, *The Merchant of Venice*

In comments to the faculty about university search committees, I
recently asked: "Can anyone recall the members of the committee
who recommended me for my position, and have they been *con-
gratulated?*"

Silence. Embarrassed laughter.

"Well," I asked, "have they been *punished?*"

No one could remember who was on the search committee.
Frankly, neither can I.[2]

SEARCHING IN ACADEME

According to McLaughlin and Riesman in their *Choosing a College
President,* about three hundred to four hundred presidential searches

take place every year—a substantial proportion of the two thousand baccalaureate granting institutions.[3] That datum is impressive enough, but multiply that by the number of searches for even shorter-lived vice-presidents, deans, department chairs—and *now* the use of full-blown search processes for virtually every position on a campus, including virtually every nonacademic manager—and you have quite an enterprise.

The purpose of the search committee is to democratize the process, to increase participation. Committees make sense for line positions with varied constituencies to serve, but the use of a committee appears to have spread to almost every position, including staff and technical jobs where the constituency may consist of one person (e.g., assistant to the dean). Too many searches are dominated not by the job to be done, but by exaggerated notions of process and fear of lawsuits.

Marchese and Lawrence, in their widely used *The Search Committee Handbook,* provide numerous useful suggestions for composing a search committee, including the wise admonition to "avoid at all costs the appointment of known paranoids, gossips and egotists. . . ."[4] I hasten to add that they recommend the appointment, rather than the election, of committee members, but I'm not sure that experience demonstrates that either election or appointment will guarantee the selection of the confident, discrete, and selfless. But it's a nice thought.

Student participation on a search committee is now assumed. My clear impression, after many years of observing students on a variety of committees, is that their influence far outweighs their rare attendance. Students on committees are listened to, responded to with care, and rarely interrupted while speaking, contrary to typical professionals' behavior toward each other. Professors, administrators, and trustees on committees fear showing any disrespect to the youth of America, so the student view almost always is recorded or noted somewhere, e.g., "The committee was unanimous, including the student member(s)."

Many faculty members persist in the great myth of university life, best described by Andrew Jackson in his great defense of the government spoils system, that administrative work is so simple that anyone can handle it. It is, indeed, remarkable that so much effort is put into filling such simple jobs. There also is a general disdain for people with degrees in "higher education," who, theoretically, are trained and educated to be higher education leaders. If that isn't funny, I don't know what is.

A measure of distrust, even a little hatred between management and labor, appears to be part of the human condition, but only in academe do the workers play a major role in choosing their own disliked managers. In their highly acclaimed study of the American professoriate, Bowen and Schuster painted a dismal portrait of a "frustrated and dispirited" faculty. They found substantial numbers of faculty do not trust administrators and "were quick to criticize campus administrators for any perceived malfeasance."[5] No study exists to determine how long it takes for distrust and enmity to set in between a college president and the faculty, but if the turnover rate for high-level academic administrators is any guide, it doesn't take long. The "charming, brilliant, and erudite" selectee of the search committee changes into "boorish, dull, and stupid" pretty fast.

A surprisingly ample amount of literature on the search process exists, proving once again academe's penchant for belaboring the obvious and publishing it in the form of books, articles, and, yes, even doctoral dissertations.[6]

A recent study of the search process contains a flowchart with twenty-four steps, including several unnumbered steps flowing from the major activities (e.g., "If no, return to step 7"). The suggested steps include admonitions to determine that a vacancy exists, to schedule meetings of the search committee (including the step "search committee convenes"), and a host of other obvious matters indicating the apparent lack of good sense of persons engaged in the search for presidents, provosts, and deans.[7]

Recruitment of educational executives once was the prerogative of trustees and/or the president. I've read several accounts of how a trustee or two would visit an unwary potential president and, after the exchange of pleasantries, offer the position to a startled, grateful, and unbelievably humble servant. This ritual now takes place through headhunter "consultants" who call or visit and make discreet inquiries. Unfortunately, the consultants cannot offer the job, but they can still make a person feel startled, grateful, and unbelievably humble.

The search consultant, long used in the corporate world, is now quite commonplace for college and university presidential searches and increasingly utilized at many other levels both academic and technical. But in academe, unlike most corporate searches, the consultant is an add-on to the regular committee, sometimes causing consternation and confusion, other times serving in most beneficial ways to calm political waters and to assuage trustees who are from the corporate world. Search consultants may be compared to other brokers—marriage, financial, real estate. If the marriage succeeds, the broker is praised; if the marriage fails, the broker is rarely remembered and *never* held responsible. Then again, neither are search committees operating on their own.

The growing list of experts in academic search all recommend that a vacancy should be used as an opportunity to reevaluate the position, including the question "Do we really need this job?" Now, I haven't done a scientific survey, but I am willing to put forth a substantial wager that the response would be "yes" in 99 percent of the cases. Nevertheless, it is a valid question. However, it should be posed this way: "If the job is abolished but the budget assigned elsewhere, can that accomplish the same task?" Again, I haven't done a scientific survey, but I am willing to wager that there will be many competitors for the spoils and the function.

AD-ING

Consultants reportedly can tap people who are content in their present jobs and, therefore, unlikely to respond to an ad in the *Chronicle of Higher Education.* The assumption appears to be that only unhappy folks read the want ads and respond to them. While this is not true, I know from experience that most respondents to ads are not even remotely qualified for the jobs.

It is surprising how many clearly unqualified people apply for positions. Often these appear to be cranks or egomaniacs. But I have perceived something else about unqualified candidates who are otherwise *compos mentis,* and it reflects unfavorably on our profession. Many people appear to feel that working in a university requires no special talents or training, especially for academically related jobs such as teaching or deaning. Hence, large numbers of retiring military officers or businessmen express their desire to "give back" to the youth in colleges and universities. "I've always wanted to teach philosophy." "I believe that my work as a manager of widget production, wherein I supervised two hundred people, makes me suitable to serve as dean of your business school." Such applications deserve short attention and quick disposal, especially when they evidence no recognition that many of us think of this as a career which requires both training and experience.

All of us read the *Chronicle* ads, either openly or secretly. If you want to drive friends berserk, give them your *Chronicle* with several ads clipped out. Most of the ads for the position of deans and above read exactly the same, even though a search committee spent many hours arguing over content. "Must be responsive to varied constituencies" is the key phrase. Now everyone who has gone beyond first grade knows from experience that this is impossible. The divorce rate alone teaches us how tough it is to be responsive to just one person.

Reading advertisements in the *Chronicle* is a fascinating exercise. Presumably, they are drafted with care, and occasionally subtle differences do emerge. These subtle differences often reveal an attempt to find a person who is unlike the last holder of the position. In such cases, emphasis is placed on personal qualities rather than specific technical talents, training, or experience. In personnel matters, I believe in the cliché that the things that count can't be counted. So I'm not impressed with most job descriptions, particularly for high-level posts. Indeed, I am most impressed with the ad I saw recently from a major university that said simply they were seeking a president. All around it were other presidential search ads of various sizes detailing all sorts of desirable characteristics, which I presume any president must have.

One could legitimately argue that jobs that can be easily described do not need a major search process. The search process should be reserved for those positions which call for such indescribable characteristics as ability to handle the unexpected and to inspire others to advance an agenda.

Search consultant Maria M. Perez wisely notes:

> Committees define what they are looking for as they begin to see résumés, even as they interview people, and they keep redefining it. Sometimes an individual walks in and he or she completely changes the definition and gets the job. So never assume you are in a process that is clear-cut and rational."[8]

Ads that read "search reopened" or "search extended" bring special delight. My imagination reviews the scenario: elaborate selection and organization of the search committee; intense discussions of criteria; broadbased field inquiries to please affirmative action officers and perhaps make the "big" catch; floods of letters, responses, résumés, references, files; excitement of the first candidate interview; increasing depression with the parade of candidates; shortlist formation; the second interview rounds; bills, expense records of lunches and dinners, airfares; and finally, either rejection by the nominee or, more likely, a weary, warring committee divided against itself.

Having survived a few of these over the years, I can tell you that the despair at the end is real. But some amusement can be derived by listening to the postmortem, which attributes the failure to the appointing officer rather than the committee or the search consultant—and never to the candidate who parlayed the offer into a higher salary to stay put.

SHH!

The dominant theme of every search (outside of the "sunshine law" jurisdictions for public institutions) is CONFIDENTIALITY. It smothers everyone. Campuses, used to openness, candid exchange, and the continuous sharing of secrets by swearing all listeners to confidentiality, generally accept the notion that search committees will not reveal anything, except in confidence. While I acknowledge the need for confidentiality for candidates whose situations elsewhere may be threatened, the fact is that confidentiality is rarely maintained at either the campus of the candidates or on the campus conducting the search. In some cases, documented by McLaughlin and Riesman, confidentiality was maintained by not bringing finalists to the campus at all! So much for the sense of community we all seek.

Ordinarily, however, information is leaked by committee members to "trusted confidants" or discovered by enterprising reporters. As the network of contacts and references widens, the holes in the dike grow more numerous. I have determined that "confidential" means telling just one person at a time, while "secret" is best conveyed by Benjamin Franklin who noted in *Poor Richard's Almanac* that "three may keep a secret, if two of them are dead." The academy should have foreseen that the cry for "open searches" would result in exhaustive efforts to be secretive about all of it or to be so open as to scare off the best candidates.

It was widely rumored on my campus that I was a finalist for a presidency of another university. I first heard it from a student (!) and next from a faculty member who heard about it from a faculty member from the other campus. The rumor was not true. When the victor was named, I received condolences as well as expressions of satisfaction that I was not leaving. I don't know quite how to classify this in the confidentiality game, but I'm not sure now whether to believe the condolers or the satisfied.

A word about "sunshine laws." These require that a search for a president be conducted in full view of the press and public. The rationale is rooted in the notion that the search is the public's business similar to that of legislative, executive, and judicial activity. The fact that most of the important parts of *those* activities take place in secret, particularly when decisions are made (e.g., conference committees in legislatures, closed executive meetings, and juries), appears to be irrelevant. Suffice it to say that experience clearly demonstrates that sunshine laws affect adversely the behavior of search committees, the quality of candidates, and the atmosphere on both the searching campus and its surrounding community and on the campus and environs of candidates. I find, after diligent consideration, absolutely no justification for sunshine laws for sensitive personnel matters and strongly recommend reliance on the usual leaking of confidential information.

When I convene a search committee, I always begin with: "Confidentiality begins right now." While I am clearly a skeptic, I confess being moved by the following tale:

> One university president allowed a search committee to put his name forward in an exploratory way. When news of his candidacy was leaked to the press, his campus and local community turned on him and his family, verbally abusing his children in school, dumping garbage on the front steps of his home, and publicly denouncing him as a traitor in the local newspapers. The situation became so ugly that he was forced to submit his resignation. When he was not the search's final choice, he found himself without a job.[9]

PAPER CHASES

Search committee members spend a lot of time reading résumés. This is an art. Rarely does a recruitment season go by when I don't review at least half a dozen résumés that are suspicious either on veracity or on emphasis. Lately, résumés seem much bulkier, much more repetitious, and much more prone to treat "letters to the editor" as major publications. Many people publish literally hundreds of things, taking numerous pages to list them. I wonder how they find time to do all that, as well as teach, read, watch television, vacation, talk to colleagues, and make love.

Behavior patterns emerge quickly on a search committee. One member swoons over application letters of six or seven single-spaced pages that depict the applicant's philosophies of life and education ("I believe most strongly in the consultative process . . ."). Another wonders openly why someone with "such excellent paper credentials" would want to leave Prestige U to come *here*. The cynic on the committee ignores the paper, waiting for the interviews ("I can spot a leader when I see one").

The contemporary résumé is done by a professional on buff paper, using all of the current buzzwords that indicate achievement: "managed," "organized," "chaired," "developed," "supervised," and (the really big one) "coordinated." Most of us are smart enough to know what most job experience entails without the assistance of descriptive words.

One of the more mysterious aspects of academic résumés is that part devoted to "service" activities. This usually appears as a list of committee assignments, leadership positions, task forces, and outside community activities. I rarely take these seriously unless buttressed by supporting data. For example, one may list membership in an academic senate or on prestigious sounding committees, but we have all observed numerous persons who either never attended a meeting of a committee or did attend every meeting and never said even one word over the span of two or three years. Yet one might assume such membership to reflect the high regard of peers and supervisors.

Letters of reference should be abolished. Most of them resemble copies of an all-purpose memo; just fill in the blanks with the date, name of applicant, and position for which he/she applied. Many people fear applicants will read letters of reference they write. I have yet to see a truly unfavorable letter, although I have seen some that, with careful reading, show imaginative, rapier-like thrusts that neatly skirt libel suits.

I recently wrote a letter on behalf of an aspiring member of my faculty, only to learn that the search committee chair returned the files of unsuccessful applicants to the applicants, including the confidential letters! When the person asked me to write for still another application, she suggested I leave out some particular (truthful) comment about her qualifications because it "weakened an otherwise good letter."

THE HOT SEAT

The interview is the high point of the process: the search committee around the table in the best conference room on campus, focused on the potential messiah who will lift the entire university—or some portion of it—from the deadweight of its past leaders (who also were recommended by a search committee).

Many interviews take place during meals. At that time the candidate is stared at by several persons at the table and is expected to: (1) answer questions, (2) order food with the quiet skill of a world traveler, and (3) chew his or her food with mouth closed while talking. Maria M. Perez, president of a search firm, observed that "the chicken and you are grilled, then they eat you for lunch." She suggests (seriously) that the candidate carry a peanut butter sandwich and consume it during a bathroom break.[10]

It is not uncommon for the search committee to seek someone who will "stand up to" the board, the vice-president, the provost, or the deans. The committee wants a leader of the opposition, an adversary to the applicant's future superior. This mind-set usually emerges in the form of snide, humorous remarks about the superior, followed by a question such as the one posed to me in an interview: "What would you do if the president wanted to overrule a faculty decision that you strongly supported?" (My response: "I would fall on my sword—and tell my wife to get a job that paid real money.")

Indeed, it is not uncommon, unfortunately, for a search to be characterized as an airing of grievances to the candidates during the on-campus interviews. "We have a totalitarian administration. Can you undo that?" "Students are never consulted here." "Would you hold open meetings of the entire faculty on all issues of importance?" Indeed, if surveys and studies such as that of Bowen and Schuster are to be believed, faculty mistrust their administrators so much that it is strange that they continue to hold out hope for the newest potential leaders. I have been amazed at how much "dirt" a candidate can uncover in the course of a day or two on a strange campus. I have experienced this as a candidate myself and as an interviewer of candidates on my home campus.

Happily, there is an ingredient in all candidates that believes they can overcome any malaise which has been revealed. Happily, there is an ingredient in search committees that presumes that the unveiling of every grievance will assure their eradication by the candidate sitting before them. I'll let the turnover rate of high-level administrators speak to that issue.

Search committee interviews can range from incisive to inane. In the course of an interview for a dean's position, a search committee member asked me what I thought about the Vietnam War. When I indicated that I considered the question puzzling, I was told, "Well, I'm just trying to see what kind of person you are."

One question often asked of candidates runs something like this: "Can you, as a scientist, appreciate and address the needs of humanists and social scientists?" Not only does the question show a misperception of administrative talent, it presumes someone actually might answer "no." My response is simple: "If you have a candidate who is experienced and conversant with all subjects, make an offer on the spot."

Search committees often contain members who don't know what the job to be filled is really about. The fact is that few people know what a university president does, or understand how a senior administrator spends the day. The litmus test for me is the number of times I have been asked, by faculty, how I spent my summer, my spring break, the month-long break between fall and spring semesters, etc. The assumption is that I am not present when they are not present. Such queries are not unlike the annual statement of my neighbor of many years, delivered each May: "Well, now you're off for three months."

The most dangerous aspect of this is that the committee may, and often does, misread the skills necessary to the task. Does that account for the high turnover of administrators or our disappointment in the performance of so many new hires? Marchese and Lawrence caution that "you are not looking for the 'most liked' candidate; you are looking for abilities matched to a post," and they wisely suggest that the shrewdest appraisal will come from those in parallel posts.[11]

Increasingly, search committees are urged to "structure" their interviews by planning a sequence of questions. This is done to be fair, to assure equality, and to avoid affirmative action pitfalls. We certainly have come a long way from the old-boy network to a time when we not only open the network and politicize the entire process, we even stage the discussion. This suggests to me that: (1) the position is so predictable in requirements as to bring the need for a search process into question, (2) that there is little understanding of the skills and experiences required for most major posts on a campus, or (3) that "fairness" and "nondiscrimination" concerns have affected our senses.

I was told of a search in which concern about equal treatment of all candidates took the form of escorting an inside candidate on the same tour of the campus given to all outside candidates. I suggested that I would have enjoyed being along on that tour since it was probably hilarious, but I was solemnly assured that nary a giggle was heard. The committee was concerned that the inside candidate might bring suit if she was not chosen (she wasn't and she didn't).

Body language and "dressing for success" are critical factors. Every search committee contains at least two experts on those subjects, one of whom (frequently a student) has read a book about such things. A few tips are in order for interviewees: Dress for the particular job, but dress well enough to show you appreciate the invitation; touching fingertips while talking is very impressive; folding arms across the chest is defensive; slouching is disrespectful, but you needn't sit as stiffly as if you were dining at West Point. The most critical body signs occur when you first enter the room. Be absolutely certain to look each person in the eye as you offer a firm handshake. Even one slip of the eye and one weak handshake may be fatal. It is commonly assumed by search consultants that the first two minutes make or break you.

Committee members often visit the campus of finalists for presidential vacancies, more rarely for deans and vice-presidents. This is enormously flattering to the applicant, even though it tends to set the applicant's campus buzzing with rumors about what was said to the visitors. Should no offer result, the applicant wonders what terrible things were said and apparently is in danger of having garbage dumped on his front steps. On the other hand, the successful applicant may find, as John Kennedy suggested, that victory has many "fathers." He or she is besieged with congratulations from 263 persons who spoke to the visitors during their four-hour stay.

Many candidates like to play "cool," acting as though they couldn't care less about getting the position. They evidence a "show me, win me" attitude. I realize that a candidate may, indeed, need to be convinced of a fit between the institutional need and him or herself, but I prefer someone who says, "I am interested. If there is a fit, I am the person you need. I am not wasting your time or mine. I am ready to move if an offer results." Recently a finalist for a deanship on my campus, who was eminently qualified, succeeded in turning off one supporter after another by making a big point of "show me, win me." When I called to tell him that he was not selected, he was quite surprised and disappointed. In fact, his disappointment was so clear that I told him why—that he made everyone feel that he would be doing us a favor by joining our ranks.

Neither side should play a show-me game because, as McLaughlin and Riesman conclude, "the final selection on both sides represents a leap of faith."[12]

INSIDE-OUTSIDE-UPSIDE DOWN

Richard Kaplowitz in his *Selecting College and University Personnel* likens the search process in higher education to a mythical journey or quest in which a treasure is gained.[13] Timothy Healy characterizes the process as "Looking for 'God on a Good Day.' "[14] There *is* a certain expectation in the early meetings of a search committee that envisions a great and noble body springing forth from the multitudes to bring some imagined new spirit to the campus. (I assume the new spirit resembles Harvard's on a good day.) Somehow, the vision never matches anyone already on campus. Even though every representation of the human/academic species can be found on any typical American campus, the feeling persists that "somewhere out there" is someone far beyond the range of anyone in town.

A former student of mine was the victor in a search for the academic vice-presidency of a regional state university. Shortly after arriving on campus, the presidency became vacant and a faculty meeting was held to discuss the forthcoming search. Several faculty members suggested seeking potential presidents from among Nobel Laureates. The new vice-president, a witty character, suggested that a good beginning would be to form a committee composed of all the Nobel Laureates on that campus! I am told that the vice-president's "honeymoon" ended right there.

A search is always more stimulating if there are viable inside candidates. This offers search committee members, as well as the whole campus, reason to discuss one of the great issues of organizational theory: inside vs. outside candidates. Sometimes the debate is not funny. The search may be an affirmative action sham to cloak an intention to appoint a specific insider. A careful watch of the *Chronicle* does show a remarkably large number of inside appointments, especially of those already holding the position as "acting." This might induce a cynical observer to smile knowingly, but it is not amusing to outside candidates who made sincere applications.

Inside candidates have a tough time for some simple reasons. First, everyone assumes that a "god for a day" is waiting to be called from the heavens above. Second, consultants, now regularly used, have to provide an extensive list from their rolodex, which would be adversely affected by a well-known insider. Third, and most important, is that while inside promotion is common in the corporate sector where the search process is less participatory, the campus constituency gets a strong voice whereby they "not only tend to undervalue those they know but have the power to act on their deprecations."[15]

The one really good thing to come out of all the tedium of search committees and the processes that characterize them is the emphasis on affirmative action for women and minorities. Nevertheless, the results do not yet warrant cheers. Affirmative action requirements haunt and challenge committees. University affirmative action officers often have substantial authority to affect the process.

That tokenism exists cannot be denied because the applicant pool must hold up in court, if not on the job. Still, it is amusing to see how a committee confronts the issue when members realize that out of 173 applications, only four white women, one black man, and two Hispanic women emerged in the first cut to twenty-five candidates. If the second cut results in one white woman, one Hispanic woman, and eight white males—with everyone's top favorites being white males—things really get interesting.

WINNERS AND LOSERS

When the committee finishes its work and submits three finalists to the appointing officer (with subtle suggestions that, while they had to submit three names, only one of the original 173 candidates is really suitable), the committee adjourns for a final drink at the pub. Any appointing officer worthy of the job rarely is surprised by the list or the subtle suggestions, but if he or she is surprised, then watch for the *Chronicle* "search reopened" ad.

Meanwhile, those candidates notified that they are finalists begin the process of making that psychological break with their present situation. They spin endless fantasies of a new life, bolstered by interminable discussions with family members and close colleagues of what to do should the offer come.

There is remarkably little attention paid in the extensive literature on search to the trauma of moving and changing jobs. Studies on stress generally list moving and job change just slightly below death of a loved one, divorce, and serious illness among life's most stressful times. Often, a job change is sought because of the breakup of a marriage or love affair or other personal crisis, which adds to the trauma. The stress felt by a successful candidate may be relatively simple compared to that felt by the spouse and children. Search consultants need to devise a series of questions to determine a candidates's capacity to handle the stress unforeseen in the euphoria of the search process.

For the winner, the impact is spontaneous on both ends: The winner quickly severs ties on the "old" campus; the impending change alters everyone's expectations and behavior on the "new" campus.

At home, the winner becomes engaged in the rites of moving and all that entails. Friends, neighbors, and colleagues begin a round of burdensome and sometimes heart-wrenching farewell parties. The winner's boss and subordinates treat him as though he were invisible. The children refuse to leave. Packing boxes becomes the stuff of life. Stress abounds.

When the move is completed, the winner finds the new campus community is not quite as anxious to please as the search committee suggested. As the winner crosses the quad, he wonders if any of the people he passes were members of the search committee.

The combination of an upset family life and a campus reception somewhat less enthusiastic than expected leaves the winner feeling somewhat isolated, wondering whether making the change was the right move. Fortunately, these feelings usually wear off within two years. Shortly after that, the now-jaded victor begins scanning the *Chronicle* once again—hmm, write to "Chair, Search Committee. . . ."

NOTES

1. Portions of this chapter were published in "Search and Ye Shall Find?" *Educational Records* 69, nos. 3–4 (Summer–Fall 1988): 48–51.

2. I do know that several members of the committee are no longer with the university. I suggest, therefore, as a topic for further research: "How many members of a search committee leave the institution before the candidate selected leaves?"

3. Judith Block McLaughlin and David Riesman, *Choosing a College President: Opportunities and Constraints* (Princeton, N.J.: The Carnegie Foundation for the Advancement of Teaching, 1990), p. xxi.

4. Theodore J. Marchese and Jane Fiori Lawrence, *The Search Committee Handbook: A Guide to Recruiting Administrators* (Washington, D.C.: American Association for Higher Education, 1987), p. 7.

5. Howard R. Bowen and Jack H. Schuster, *American Professors: A National Resource Imperiled* (New York: Oxford University Press, 1986), p. 140.

6. See the bibliographies compiled in Richard A. Kaplowitz, *Selecting College and University Personnel: The Quest and the Questions,* ASHE-ERIC Higher Education Report No. 8 (Washington, D.C.: Association for the Study of Higher Education, 1986), and in McLaughlin and Riesman.

7. Kaplowitz, pp. 10–11.

8. Theodore J. Marchese, "Search from the Candidate's Perspective: An Interview with Maria M. Perez." *American Association for Higher Education Bulletin* 42, no. 4 (December 1989): p. 5.

9. Judith Block McLaughlin, "From Secrecy to Sunshine: An Overview of Presidential Search Practice." *Research in Higher Education* 22, no. 2 (1985): p. 206.

10. Marchese, p. 11.

11. Marchese and Lawrence, pp. 44–45.

12. McLaughlin and Riesman, p. xxxiii.

13. Kaplowitz, p. 1.

14. Timothy S. Healy, "Looking for 'God on a Good Day.' " *Association of Governing Boards of Universities and Colleges Reports* 27, no. 2 (1985): p. 22.

15. McLaughlin and Riesman, p. 243.

5

What to Look for in a Candidate

M. Fredric Volkmann

Finding the right person in a job search is a little like Terman's Law of Innovation: "If you want a track team to win the high jump, you find one person who can jump seven feet, not seven people who can each jump one foot."[1]

While this may seem like stating the obvious, we have only to look around university campuses to quickly discover that Terman's Law has not been uniformly applied. Finding the person who can make these seven-foot accomplishments is essential at all levels of institutional operation. The trick is locating and attracting candidates who fill such needs.

Regrettably, there is virtually no training easily available on how to locate the best candidates, screen them, conduct effective interviews, assess and measure positive and negative qualities, and thoroughly check credentials. Compounding this is the increasingly contentious and sometimes litigious atmosphere in which the interviewing and screening process must operate.

Although a simpler but expensive solution may be the use of a head-hunting firm to handle these matters, it is the purpose of this chapter to suggest guidelines helpful to those who conduct their own searches. Before beginning the interview phase of any search, contact your personnel or human resources office for advice, legal counsel, and their policies and procedures. Institutions generally have precise and prescribed steps that must be followed. These steps may not help you with all phases of the process, but they are designed to keep you out of serious legal and affirmative action difficulty. With that said, the burden of responsibility for a successful search falls on you and how well you have screened the finalists.

HOW TO FIND THE BEST APPLICANTS

A formal search process involves certain actions that must be uniformly followed, regardless of institutions and their policies. Unfortunately, these efforts may not bear the best results and can only form the bureaucratic base for what must eventually become a creative endeavor. It is critical that a search plan be developed and that minimum criteria established by the institution be met. These requirements involve such actions as notifying trade and professional association placement offices, placement offices at other colleges and universities (including historically minority institutions), advertising in majority and minority publications, and keeping accurate records of all such actions.

All of these efforts will not necessarily turn up the best candidates. The reasons are fairly simple: Unhappy people often look for new jobs, and happy ones often do not. Searching for someone who will adequately fill a position may entail greater personal contact with persons who are infinitely satisfied with their current positions and who never dreamed of considering an offer from another institution or possibilities for additional challenges. It is in this arena that one usually finds the strongest applicants and spends the greatest amount of time convincing these individuals that it is worthwhile to proceed with an application and perhaps an interview process.

Locating such candidates can be done in a number of ways, beginning with networking. When a new search is contemplated, a plan approved, and announcements sent, then is the time to get on the telephone and call the leading experts, gurus, and respected authorities in the field or discipline involved. While almost every search involves sending out query letters with an announcement and a job description, these do not have the same effect as a phone call. For every ten phone calls perhaps only one or two names will surface as serious possibilities, because often the best individuals are known to many and only a few fine possibilities rise to the surface. Critical to this process is a clearly worded and definitive description of the position and the expectations involved. Of even greater help will be any plans or strategies that define the direction or goals being set by the division (or being initiated by the division itself with the support of the leadership of your institution).

When seeking names, it is critical that sensitivity and consideration always be given toward meeting affirmative action goals, and at the same time finding persons who can successfully perform in the position. As you develop a shortlist of strong possibilities, be sure to satisfy the institution's requirements and those of the state. It must never be assumed that direct, proactive behaviors are in any way an attempt to circumvent or diminish the importance of giving every candidate an equal opportunity. In fact, this should enhance minority recruitment.

Generally, networking will develop at least six to ten strong possibilities who most likely will not respond to any advertisements or to any other mass communications initiatives announcing the position. This means that you must call these prospects, provide them with information, and convince them that there is reason to seriously consider the importance of applying for the position. At the same time, you must carefully screen all other applicants to be sure that no possibility is overlooked. Everyone's résumé or vita, and any supporting credentials, must be given equal consideration and must be viewed specifically to see if they meet the criteria established for the position.

As important as networking, but not often as productive, are several other areas of inquiry for candidates. Advertising is not just putting a notice in the local paper, or meeting obligatory affirmative action guidelines by inserting an announcement in such highly regarded publications as the *Chronicle of Higher Education*. Of perhaps even greater importance are the newsletters, placement services, and other communications of professional societies, as well as careful checking of past advertisements for searches conducted for similar positions by other institutions. For example, if you are searching for a chief financial officer for the institution or the dean of a professional school, check all of the advertisements run between one and four months earlier in the *Chronicle of Higher Education* at institutions whose programs are roughly parallel to the goals of your institution. Call those institutions and inquire as to whether the search has been completed. If it has, ask the chair of the search committee or the responsible hiring officer if they would mind sharing with you the names of candidates who were strong finalists or who were strongly courted but decided either not to apply or to accept an offer. Once you have this list of names, do some further checking with your network about those individuals and then decide whether to contact any new names that have shown up. This "reverse review" of prior advertisements helps you benefit from the screening and interviewing efforts already conducted by similar institutions. However, be aware that some states may restrict what candidate-search information can be shared with other institutions, including names.

Although a strong résumé or an outstanding vita from an unknown candidate may signal a "dark-horse candidate" who deserves attention, it is critical that all candidates be asked to submit additional material substantiating their abilities, program success, or potential. While some institutions and states have specific regulations about what can be requested on the initial contact with candidates, it is critical that manuscripts, writing samples, proof of creative ability, or any other examples be submitted as early as possible, so that your rating and screening will be more easily accomplished. As a practice, do not begin any interview process until after the announced application deadline for the position has passed, and all pertinent materials are received from candidates who appear to have possibilities.

Job searches today will result in literally hundreds of inquiries. Therefore, a systematic method of keeping track of credentials and other materials is vital and requires a strongly sensitive, reactive effort to notify all candidates that materials have been received and that gives some clue as to the candidate's potential for success. One of the most common methods of doing so is creating a file folder for each inquiry into which all materials are placed, including copies of reply correspondence from the institution. Then, as materials are received, the candidate should receive a letter within ten days produced on a word-processing or other labor-saving device that clearly establishes some sense of the future of the applicant's position in the search process.

The most successful candidates are those who clearly meet all of the job description criteria, who have had successful roles at other institutions, and whose salary expectations are clearly within the ability of the searching institution to pay. Not only should they receive a letter, but also should be called by phone to continue cultivating their interest.

The second category of candidates are those who clearly meet the minimum requirements, but whose track records are not as well established and whose potential for success may not be as high. Their letter should be businesslike, but not overly encouraging.

The third category are those candidates whose credentials simply do not meet the minimum qualifications. These individuals should receive a letter announcing their failure to meet minimum requirements and wishing them success in whatever other endeavors they may have in mind.

As one dean at a major research university said, "I classify staff and faculty in three categories—superstars, journeymen, and duds." Be sure that your superstar prospects receive continuing indications of your great pleasure at their interest in the position. The best combination is a carefully crafted letter, followed by a personal telephone call making it clear to the individual that he or she is among that highly select group of candidates who "have made the final cut toward the interview process."

Depending upon the candidate's willingness to have his or her interest in the position known to others, it is important to thoroughly check the credentials and the past work history of the individual. For those candidates who wish to keep their availability confidential, this becomes a ticklish situation that may require either complete adherence to the candidate's wishes or a very careful analysis of the individual's background without alerting anyone to the candidate's involvement. This is where networking becomes particularly important. Equally critical is knowing whom to call in reviewing those candidates who are less reluctant to have their availability known.

Calling references from the candidate's supplied list may not be the best source of information on the applicant's real potential. If there is an extensive work record, contacting supervisors in previous positions to the one currently held by the individual can be helpful, particularly if the currently held position is less than three years old.

Ultimately, every institution should insist on speaking to its top finalist's supervisor prior to final hiring, regardless of the reasons the employee may express for not doing so. This, of course, would not happen until it was clear there was a single finalist who would be offered the position and whose bona fides must be checked out in detail. (The ideal situation is the candidate whose current supervisor is open-minded about the advancement of his or her own staff and who is able to handle the knowledge that a current employee is being sought by others. Contacting this individual will usually provide the best, up-to-date information on how well the candidate will fit into your environment.)

ANALYZING THE COVERING LETTER, RÉSUMÉ, AND ANY SUPPORTING MATERIAL

An application for a position should be an exercise not only in good self-marketing, but also in honesty, integrity, and accuracy. Whether intentional or otherwise, this is not always the case. First, be absolutely certain that there are no errors in the covering letter or the résumé/vita of the candidate. If there are glaring errors in spelling, punctuation, usage, or other areas relating to accuracy, careful consideration should be given to removing the candidate from your final list. Most people have little patience for error in something so important, and academe does not offer sanctuary to those who cannot master the language nor provide good detailed reporting of information. Furthermore, mistakes on vital papers by the candidate may indicate future problems with the individual's attention to critical details within the classroom or office environment. Accepting little mistakes at the outset may lead to trying to solve much bigger ones later on.

Analyzing the credentials of applicants must be handled quite differently, based on whether the individual is filling a faculty or administrative role. Faculty positions rely heavily on proof of education, publications, and other teaching and research credentials that show preparation, potential, and familiarity with the currently held views and perspectives within the discipline. Administrative positions, on the other hand, can take on a much different set of requirements often focused heavily on experience in similar roles at other institutions. Receiving a six- to ten-page vita from a prospect for a presidency, a deanship, or a faculty position is quite appropriate, but one of that length for an administrative position in advancement, finance, or student affairs may be completely inappropriate. Being "credential-happy" has two totally different meanings, depending upon the position being filled.

Just as there are clear signals as to someone's competency in an academic setting based on where the person was educated, the quality and depth of his or her publications, and presentations made before colleagues at major meetings, so can there be a clear ability to "read the tea leaves" for administrative prospects. However, administrators have to be judged on other qualities than simply having the right array of academic proofs to support his or her candidacy. This is where careful checking on the individual with previous supervisors is vital. Résumés for administrators provide far fewer clues for potential success than do those for members of the faculty.

Length of service in prior positions is a vital concern. Applicants who have had three or more jobs in the last five years may be providing ample warning as to whether they will be employed very long at your institution as well. Look cautiously at those who have the potential for future job-hopping or who may not find it easy to fit within a specific environment, no matter how outstanding his or her credentials may be. Look also at the résumé for some proof of a well-rounded personality who has interests beyond a very narrow academic or administrative role. Absence of proof may not be an indication of a problem but can suggest if the individual will have the breadth of character to lead, rather than follow. Check to see if there is a steady progression of promotions and expanded responsibilities.

Covering letters can be quite revealing as to the potential of a candidate. Look for willingness as opposed to excuses, positive point of view rather than reserved or negative, and awareness of the institution to which the candidate is applying. Persons who show an ability to overcome adversity to serve their clientele or students and who become genuinely interested in the institution that employs them are more likely to be successful than those who take on a "hire-me-before-some-other-lucky-place-gets-me" attitude. Letters and résumés that oversell, overstate, or oversimplify should be clear warnings to the interviewer and the search committee. Caution is advised for those candidates who suggest or allude to some of the following:

- "I'll take the job regardless of salary."

- "I know I've moved around a lot, but I'm ready to settle down."

- "I'll take a cut in pay to work for you."

- "I know I've had problems in the past, but I've reformed and know now how to deal with my weaknesses."

- "I'm finally straightening out my personal life and know this job will be a great help in completing that process."

- "Please don't contact any of my previous employers."

- "I need a change in career path, and you seem to be the best thing I've seen yet."

Be careful with those candidates who ask too quickly about salaries, benefits, or other bottom-line issues before inquiring about the challenge the position offers and the opportunities to grow in the role.

Lastly, be certain to carefully check through any samples or reference to materials submitted by the applicant. If you are using a search committee, ask committee members to review materials carefully to be sure they are completely original and show mastery of the discipline or administrative area involved. If you are not using a search committee, ask a member of the staff to review the supporting materials of your top finalists for the same reasons. While plagiarism and other examples of academic dishonesty are rarely found, this problem requires greater vigilance to protect the institution from any future embarrassment. Where questions are raised in checking supporting materials, it is best to ask the candidate directly, unless there is blatant evidence of unwarranted borrowing of information or "creative" completion of other details in work history or in publishing. The above may be substantial grounds for not considering a candidate, and warning signals do have value in forcing a deeper probe into the candidate's background. Today, it is easier to not hire than to fire.

THE GIVE AND TAKE OF INTERVIEWING

University consultant Arthur Ciervo[2] once said, "The basic difficulty of the interview, as usually conducted, is that it involves making extensive inferences from limited data obtained in artificial situations by unqualified observers." He goes on to note that too much is expected from an interview, and too much attention is, therefore, given to a single clue or to an insufficent number of clues. He suggests an interview should serve only three basic purposes: (1) to obtain information, (2) to give information, and (3) to make a friend for the institution.

Even if limited in its value, the interview may be the most critical aspect in determining who will or will not be a successful candidate for your opening. There is vital information to be gleaned and imparted during the process, especially if it is wisely and strategically structured. Regardless of whether a search committee or single-manager decision is undertaken, it is critical that the candidate not be mistreated or mishandled in the process. For example, subjecting an applicant to a series of group interviews, rather than one-on-one interviews, may not produce vital information, simply because this interpersonal dynamic is not typical of how people work on an hour-by-hour basis. Setting up a series of seven or eight 30- to 60-minute interviews can often be more valuable than two or three group interviews in the same time frame.

No matter which approach is taken, it is vital that those conducting the interview have complete information about each candidate, including a résumé or vita, copies of any appropriate correspondence, and samples the individual has submitted of work that can be inexpensively and easily copied for distribution. Try to be sure that the persons interviewing each candidate are the same throughout the search, so that ample opportunity exists for fair comparison by each interviewer between the interviewed finalists.

Before any interviews take place, assure yourself and your colleagues that you each know what you and the institution are looking for and how best you can determine those qualities. As the actual interview unfolds, take time to develop a strong sense of rapport. A warming-up process is critical to establishing what can be an uncomfortable experience for both applicant and interviewer. Don't be concerned about nervousness, since this affects a high number of people. Besides, few applicants have had much experience at being interviewed.

Be certain that the interview operates at an informal level. For example, don't sit across a desk or table from the candidate. Instead, arrange your office or interview environment so that you are sitting at a round table or across the corner of a desk, or simply sitting in two chairs facing each other. The hint of barriers can reduce the candor and the sense of free exchange that benefit the interview process.

Remember that one of the primary purposes of the interview is to exchange information. To do so, this requires skillful questions that elicit more than a "yes" or "no" response from the candidate. Among the questions you should consider asking are the following, asking for examples of how the candidate handles each situation you have brought up:

- "Tell me in your own words why you are interested in this position."

- "What do you like least (best) about your present position?"

- "I've noticed that you used to work for (name of institution), and I wonder if you could tell me why you left that position for the one you hold now?"

- "Who was the best boss or mentor you ever had? Why? Was there one you didn't like? Would you tell me why?"

- "How well do you set priorities for your work and follow them?"

- "What level of productivity (quantity of work) do you exhibit?"

- "How effective are you in long-range (annual) planning of your responsibilities and tasks?"

- "How effective are you in short-term (daily and weekly) planning of projects and tasks?"

- "How effectively do you delegate tasks to others, when appropriate?"

- "How successfully have you mastered and then utilized computer and other essential communications technology that are a part of office or classroom routine?"
- "Tell me about your strongest points and give me some examples."
- "Can you share with me any weaknesses you feel you have that deserve greater attention?"
- "How well do you take suggestions or direction from senior colleagues or supervisors?"

A critical section of the interview is assessing skills and habits. Following is a technique that can be helpful in getting to know the candidate's self-perceptions: "I'm going to list some qualities on which I would like you to give me a grade or assessment of your skills. Please tell me how you rate yourself on a scale of 5 (excellent) to 1 (poor) on the following attributes:

- Writing assigned or research material;
- Speaking extemporaneously before audiences, including classes and colleagues;
- Presenting formal lectures to peers in your discipline;
- Editing copy produced by others;
- Meeting deadlines agreed upon earlier;
- Working in a team with colleagues and subordinates;
- Managing other people (if this is appropriate to the position that you are seeking);
- Keeping a good schedule and coming to work at reasonable times;
- Effectively utilizing your time;
- Being a self-starter;
- Being helpful to others when they need it; and
- Dealing with criticism of your work or output by superiors or senior colleagues."

At the end of the interview, consider asking: "If money and personal or professional obligations were no issue, what would you prefer doing five years from now?" The answer may provide insight into whether the individual sees your opening as a true opportunity.

The subject of grading one's self may not always be a good idea, based upon the position being filled. However, it is invaluable when dealing in managerial roles that involve such activities as editing, writing, accounting, other business procedures, and management of important or sensitive information.

As a rule, most applicants will honestly answer your questions, so do not be too concerned if there are slight discrepancies between answers to similar questions. If a strongly inconsistent pattern emerges, however, then more careful checking of credentials should be considered.

Obviously, there are many other questions that should be asked if there are unanswered matters supplied with the résumé or the supporting materials. For example, you are perfectly free to inquire about why there are gaps in employment history, attempts to blame others for failures mentioned by the candidate during the interview, or excessive complaining or boasting emerging during the give-and-take.

During the interview be careful not to take too many notes, if at all possible. Instead, try to keep a running mental account of your answers and questions and write them down immediately following the departure of the candidate from your office or the meeting area. Keeping a running tally during an interview process can be unnecessarily intimidating for those who are unaccustomed to a thoroughgoing interview process. Documentation is essential and careful records can prove helpful in recommending a successful applicant, as well as in recalling details at a future time.

Remember that you are looking for "value-added" qualities— not just specific details or minutiae about the candidate. The interview session should eventually reveal how strongly the candidate seeks to excel, wants to work productively, shows enthusiasm, and exhibits a willingness to exert energy in doing so. That said, there are danger signals that sometimes surface during interviews. According to Ciervo these include the following:

- Overqualified or overeducated for the position;

- I'll-take-anything attitude;

- Unnecessary references to personal problems;

- Slowness in responding to questions;

- Complaints about former employers or unhappiness in current position;

- Asking questions regarding salary and benefits too quickly;

- Telling the potential employer what he or she wants out of the position;

- Too talkative;

- Lack of preparation for the interview (i.e., did not bother to learn about the institution beforehand, failed to bring requisite samples, etc.);

- No display of enthusiasm;

- Credential-happy; and

- Easily intimidated.

Additional to these danger signals, look for whether or not the individual is a "playback artist" who repeats back to you what you may have indicated you want to hear. Flattery may puff up the interviewer, but it does not reveal anything about the candidate's potential for the position in showing independent or team-sensitive judgment. For such positions as editing, specialized writing, or financial management positions, you may want to consider a standardized test to determine accuracy, speed, and understanding of style and basic "rules of the trade." Before conducting such tests, be sure to check to see if state laws or institutional policies allow testing of applicants other than by the personnel office itself.

As the interview process unfolds, be sure that the interviewer does most of the listening and the candidate most of the talking. Appearing to oversell a position or talking too much about the program and its strengths cannot only be unnecessarily intimidating to candidates; it also blocks any opportunity to uncover information previously not provided. Most importantly, avoid any trickery or tactics that test the individual's ability to handle stress or surprises.

On occasion, interviews have been staged so that prearranged interruptions occur just to see how the candidate handles the situation.
These are not only unethical, but do not necessarily replicate real-
time experiences on the job.

At the end of the interview process, ask each search committee
member or interviewer individually to rank each of the applicants,
rating his or her qualifications, strengths and weaknesses, poise or
presence, and perceived capabilities. Some institutions ask that an
actual grade or ranking be given on predetermined qualities for each
of the interviewed candidates.

QUESTIONS YOU CANNOT ASK AND
INFORMATION YOU CANNOT SEEK

Although sharing information is a vital aspect of interviews and
collecting applications, state and federal laws protecting privacy and
individual rights restrict institutions and interviewers from access to
specific kinds of information. Be aware that the affirmative action
officer can request routine, voluntary information from candidates
that is not made available to interviewers nor that interviewers are
allowed to seek. For example, you cannot ask an applicant where
he or she was born or where relatives such as a spouse, parents,
or others were born. It is equally illegal to ask an applicant to disclose
his or her ancestry or national origin.

Other information the applicant is not required to supply and
that you may not require of him or her is as follows:

- You cannot ask an applicant whose name has been changed
  what his or her original name was.

- An applicant does not have to reveal his or her age unless
  it is relevant to the job—such as being of legal age to serve
  alcoholic beverages.

- As a rule, it is, therefore, usually inappropriate to see a birth
  certificate.

- A person's religion is a private matter, and you should not inquire as to name of church, parish, pastor, or even religious holidays a prospect observes.

- Citizenship is also protected and you, therefore, cannot inquire whether an applicant, his or her spouse, or parents are naturalized or native-born Americans. Nor can you ask for the dates when they might have become citizens. All you can ask is whether he or she is authorized or has a legal right to remain or work in the United States.

- It is also illegal to require an applicant to produce naturalization papers.

- Information on relatives, such as place of residence for spouse, parents, or other close relatives, is illegal, and a male applicant cannot be asked about the maiden name of his wife or mother.

- While it is appropriate to inquire as to the applicant's military service within the United States Armed Forces, it is illegal to do so regarding foreign military service.

- Applicants do not have to supply military discharge papers before employment because they show restricted information such as birthdate, place of birth, etc.

- Questions regarding membership in organizations that would disclose such information or indicate religion, race, or national origin are inappropriate.

- Not only is it illegal to ask about an applicant's race or color, but it is also inappropriate to require a photograph with the application.

- Any questions regarding marital status are unacceptable, including whether the applicant for employment prefers such titles as Miss, Ms., or Mrs.

There is information that candidates can be required to reveal. This information should be collected under personnel guidelines. For example: you can require an applicant to tell you his or her address, whether or not he or she has been convicted of a crime, whether or not the individual has had schooling and how much, prior work experience, personal character, and gender if it meets bona fide qualifications such as being a model or being an actress or actor.

Remember, these are only examples drawn from a wide range of antidiscrimination rules. You may want to check specific details in your own state by writing to the appropriate agencies or by consulting with your personnel office or institutional attorney.

CULTIVATING THE BEST CANDIDATES

When you have selected your best finalists for an opening, remember that giving information may be more important than receiving it. Deciding on a new position, often in a new location, is daunting to the best of us, particularly if there are others who will be affected by long-distance moves. Taking special steps to ease any doubt or difficulty is always appreciated by your best applicants.

After the initial application is received and it is clear that you have a few really strong individuals, be sure not only to send them appropriate letters and make personal phone calls, but then send a "care" package of information on the institution, the community, and the region. Be sure to include human resources information on benefits and policies. No interview should take place without a candidate's having had ample opportunity to learn more about the institution, its mission, its programs, and its outstanding individuals.

Included should be the most recent annual report for the institution, for the school or division involved, and even a departmental review, if available and not restricted in its circulation. Also helpful are fact brochures; recruitment materials used in selecting undergraduate, graduate, and professional students; copies of write-ups and ratings produced in the various college guides (*Fiske, Yale Daily News, Barron's, Peterson's,* and *The College Board*) for which you have copyright permission; and even copies of clippings from major popular magazines and newspapers about the institution and the program involved.

From the community surrounding the campus should come basic information from the Chamber of Commerce, real estate brochures produced by relocation agencies and realtors, information on schools, transportation, taxes, cost of living, museums and cultural entertainment, sports, and public recreation. Be sure to state your policies on paying moving expenses, transportation, and related costs.

The second stage of cultivation involves structuring of interview schedules with sufficient time to tour the campus and the community. Even on the first round of interviews, candidates should regularly be shown around the institution and offered the chance to learn at least a little bit about the surrounding area. By the second interview, the candidate should be offered the opportunity to bring a significant other (preferably at your expense) to take a day or two to investigate the area more thoroughly. Many institutions have arranged with relocation and real estate firms to have an agent take this individual through the neighborhoods and suburbs to help them get a sense not only for the housing market, but also for shopping, transportation, and basic conveniences. And if a third interview is contemplated, at least a full day should be planned for the candidate to join his or her significant other in looking over what was discovered on the second visit.

Because location and environment play such a strong role in career decisions, it is even helpful to establish job searches at optimum times. For example, one major west coast university regularly waits for the worst months of winter to interview candidates from the east coast, bringing them to the sunny shores of the Pacific at a time when they and their families are highly vulnerable. It is equally wise not to conduct interviews when it is clear that your area will be suffering its worst summer heat or the depths of a depressing winter.

MAKING YOUR FINAL DECISION
ON THE SUCCESSFUL CANDIDATE

Making the final decision must be as systematic as the preliminary efforts at collecting information on each candidate. First, recontact each of the persons who interviewed the candidates and ask for specific details in addition to any "grades" they may have assigned to each applicant they interviewed. Be certain to be fair and to have some systematic method of keeping track of comparative qualities. Don't ignore "hunches." If a majority of the interviewers share a point of view or a feeling about a candidate, pay attention.

Remembering Terman's Law, you can always find someone who can do the basic job, but what you are really after is that person who can make the quantum jumps into new levels of effectiveness and performance. The key ingredient is what Richard Irish calls "flair factors." As he says in his book *If Things Don't Improve Soon, I May Ask You To Fire Me,* a flair factor is "that vital talent, skill, capacity, orientation, or ineffable intangible without which no candidate no matter how well recommended or otherwise qualified can succeed on the job." No one clue will necessarily unveil these flair factors, but do determine how eager the candidate is to work for you and your institution. Did you notice what kind of reaction the applicant displayed to difficult questions or to things that really excited him or her about the position? What is your assessment of the candidate's accomplishments after talking with the individual and reviewing the material? And most importantly, was the applicant looking for, as Irish wisely notes, a "mission" or a "meal ticket"?

As you analyze the supporting materials from the candidate, be careful to double-check all of the factual information, such as education, work history, and special interests. Although deception is a rare problem, it is important to protect yourself and your institution against those who may be less honest in their self-characterization.

Do begin a thorough effort at checking out references from previous employers and colleagues who have a firsthand awareness of the individual and how he or she operated in a previous environment. Be careful not to focus just on those references listed by the candidate, especially if they do not include supervisors or immediate colleagues. In all cases, insist on the candidate's permission to talk to his or her immediate supervisor and to any prior supervisors.

The questions you should ask may prove troublesome. This is a time when references are not as easily forthcoming because of regulations within each institution to protect itself against legal action by current and former employees who believe they have been inappropriately rated in their performance or who wish to have information concealed.

Open the conversation with the reference by clearly identifying yourself, carefully describing the position, and reading the job description, if necessary. The questions that should be asked of the former supervisor can include the following (after assuring the individual you are calling that his or her comments will remain confidential to the best possible extent).

- Ask the former supervisor to talk to you in general about the candidate, explaining that you are not attempting to employ the perfect employee, but rather someone who can learn and grow with the program you manage.

- Ask for the strong qualities of the candidate, such as what kind of self-starter is the individual? How well does he or she work under pressure? Attitude? Willingness to take on new duties or responsibilities?

- Verify data reported on the résumé.

- After these preliminaries ask how effective the candidate is.

- One of the key questions you need answered is, "Would you hire this person for the position I have described to you? Why or why not?"

- Then ask the former supervisor if he or she would rehire this individual for the same position that they had when working at his or her institution.

Close out the interview by asking if there is anything else you should know about the applicant that would be helpful in determining his or her appropriateness for the position you are attempting to fill.

Regardless of the approach used to select the candidate, such as a search committee or a series of interviews, these questions must be asked by the hiring supervisor, and not by others. It is also critical that the information remain confidential and that the candidate's rights be protected at all times. Beware of the candidate who does not wish you to talk to his or her current supervisor or seems hesitant in your doing so. Before making the call, be sure to talk with the candidate about an appropriate way to let the supervisor know that one of his or her staff is being candidated elsewhere. It is always better if the employee makes the announcement to his or her current manager, rather than a call coming out of the blue from you.

Now you are in a position to make the decision as to who will be the successful candidate. It is critical that the job offer be made explaining what you expect of the applicant, what kind of short- and long-range goals you have established for him or her, and that you have communicated basic standards of performance consistently. Unfortunately, no matter how many safeguards and procedures are carefully followed, you have no guarantee that the right decision has been made. That comes only from a little luck and solid management principles employed in the initial experiences of the successful candidate in your new position.

NOTES

1. Frederick E. Terman, Provost Emeritus, Stanford University, quoted in Thomas L. Martin, Jr., *Malice in Blunderland* (New York: McGraw-Hill, 1973).

2. Lectures presented at the CASE Summer Institutes in Communication 1980–83, University of Notre Dame.

6

The Cost of Hiring

Lewis C. Solmon and Cheryl L. Fagnano

THE PROJECTED FACULTY SHORTAGE

For the past few years there has been considerable speculation in academic circles regarding the coming shortage of college and university faculty. It has been assumed that the combination of the large faculty cohort hired in the 1950s and 1960s that will soon be ready to retire, plus the decline in Ph.D. production in the 1970s and 1980s, will leave a dearth of highly qualified faculty. This shortage has now been confirmed in the 1989 study "Prospects for Faculty in the Arts and Sciences" by William G. Bowen and Ann Sosa.

Bowen and Sosa projected that as we go through the decade, the ratio of Ph.D. candidates to job openings will decline steadily. A ratio of 1.3 candidates per opening is considered ideal in most industries. Given the projections, this ideal ratio will not be possible for at least 10 to 15 years. For example, across all disciplines between 1987 and 1992 a ratio of 1.6 Ph.D. candidates to each faculty position was projected. Between 1997 and 2002 the ratio is expected to drop to 0.83 candidates per position. When looked at by discipline, it is clear that the shortages in some fields will be drastic. For the years 1987 through 1992, the Ph.D. candidates to faculty openings ratio was projected to be 0.71 in the humanities and social sciences, 0.80 in mathematics and the physical sciences, and 1.13 in the biological sciences and psychology (Bowen and Sosa 1989).

In terms of minority hiring, there is already an acute shortage with little prospect of improvement. In 1986 minority students represented 18 percent of the total college-going population (Mooney 1989). However, minority faculty (including non-U.S. citizens) held only 10 percent of the nation's full-time faculty positions in 1985. In 1988, the last year for which we have accurate figures, the production of minority Ph.D.s was dismal. In that year, 23,172 students received Ph.D. degrees; of these only 805 (3.5 percent) were African-American, 93 (or .4 percent) were American Indian, 612 (or 2.6 percent) were Asian, and 594 (or 2.6 percent) were Hispanic. The figures for the African-Americans are particularly worrisome because they represent a 22 percent decline during the previous ten years (Mooney 1989). Disaggregated by field, the problem intensifies. For example, between 1974 and 1987 the absolute number of Black Ph.D.s who received their degree in physical science went from 46 to 29, in engineering from 16 to 12, and in education from 501 to 379 (Solmon and Wingard 1990). In 1988 only 4 Blacks were known to have received their Ph.D.s in mathematics, according to the American Mathematical Society and the Mathematical Association of America (Mooney 1989).

HIRING WILL BE MORE DIFFICULT AND MORE EXPENSIVE

If Bowen and Sosa's projection proves accurate, hiring faculty for colleges and universities will become both more difficult and more expensive over the next decade and a half. However, the degree of difficulty in hiring will not be uniform across all disciplines or for all schools. Additional factors beyond gross supply and demand also will influence both the compensation faculty receive as well as an institution's ability to hire quality faculty in the coming years.

On the supply side, the cost of hiring will depend upon whom is hired, in what field, and from which school they graduated. On the demand side, the cost of hiring will be strongly influenced by which institution is doing the hiring, where it is located, and what resources it is able to expend on the recruitment and hiring process. Additionally, industry, professional practice, and to some extent government service, which already compete with universities for highly qualified doctorates in fields such as economics, business, engineering, computer science, law, and medicine will continue to exacerbate the problem. The level and intensity of this competition are not expected to decline in the next decade.

NOT ALL PH.D.S ARE CREATED EQUAL

At least in terms of salary and the ability to command resources, i.e., research space, equipment, and support personnel, there is considerable variation among faculty recruits. Highest on the list of desirable faculty hires are the proven academic "stars." These are typically research university faculty who bring in large grants or who have received outstanding recognition for their work. For example, any university would welcome a Nobel Laureate as a faculty member. Such individuals bring prestige to a school, which in turn is thought to attract high quality students, additional resources, and community attention and respect. Consequently, such individuals are able to command the highest salaries and the most resources. In the second tier are proven scholars, individuals known to be outstanding in their fields. The desirability of these first two levels of faculty generally cuts across discipline lines; a Nobel Laureate in literature is probably as much in demand as is one in physics or economics.

But it is not only established experts for whom schools compete; promising young professors from high prestige universities such as Harvard, Chicago, Stanford, MIT, or Berkeley are also highly sought after. There has been quite a bit written regarding the market-induced "salary compression" that arises when incoming young scholars are able to command higher salaries than some senior faculty. Such compression causes considerable morale problems among a group that ideally will work closely as collaborators and colleagues. However, this competition will in all likelihood increase if the absolute number of Ph.D.s being awarded by research universities continues to decline (Fiske 1989).

For the last six years, engineering faculty have commanded the highest salaries among all college and university professors (Blum 1989). High salaries are available in the private sector to engineers with only a bachelor's or master's degree. Due to the resultant high opportunity costs associated with doctoral study, there has been a relatively small pool of engineering Ph.D.s, and of that group only a very small percentage choose college teaching as a career. According to the *Digest of Educational Statistics,* in 1986–87 only 25.1 percent of Ph.D. engineers were planning on college teaching as a profession. This figure, while low, was actually up from 22.6 percent in 1972–73 (National Center for Educational Statistics, 1989).

Bowen and Sosa's findings suggest that the shortage will not remain limited to a few highly technical fields. Shortages are expected also to begin appearing in the humanities and social sciences. Indeed, by 1987 the number of Ph.D. graduates in the humanities, life sciences, physical sciences, social sciences, and mathematics who were planning on college teaching careers had dropped substantially from 1972. Consequently, while there has always been a salary differential according to discipline, the number of fields that will be able to command higher salaries may be increasing.

Finally, there is a new group of faculty for whom the competition to hire is intense. Schools wishing to diversify their faculty, and thereby make their institutions more hospitable to an increasingly diverse student body, are anxiously trying to outbid one another for minority Ph.D.s. As the statistics provided above show, this problem is particularly difficult and is expected to continue. Although the percentage of American Indian, Asian, and Hispanic hires increased dramatically, up 55, 57, and 26 percent respectively over the 10-year period, between 1978 and 1988 the absolute numbers were so low to begin with that the shortage continues to be acute. What these figures mean in practical terms is that currently universities and colleges are simply bidding against one another for the few minority scholars in the pool. Given the length of time it takes to produce a Ph.D., the pool is not increasing rapidly enough to meet demand. Consequently, while there is a shortage among all professors, clearly the shortage may be the most intractable among minority scholars. And this is occurring at a time when pressure to hire minorities is immense.

NOT ALL COLLEGES AND UNIVERSITIES ARE CREATED EQUAL

Like individual scholars, there is considerable variation in the "marketability" of different colleges and universities. Simply put, some schools will have an edge over others in the competition to attract faculty applicants. A prestigious name, an extensive resource base (in terms of both finances and scholarship), geographic location, quality-of-life issues, and cost of living in the area all affect the desirability of a college or university as an employer. It may be the case that candidates will require more or less monetary compensation depending upon the desirability of the hiring institution, which in turn is a function of the resources that exist there.

Other things equal, the 20 to 25 colleges and universities in the United States thought to be the top schools have an edge over lesser known institutions in the competition for faculty. Given a choice of positions providing the same total compensation, it would not be surprising if more faculty applicants selected Harvard, Stanford, or Berkeley over other high quality but less prestigious institutions. In one sense, the very best departments can offer lower salaries and still hire because those who are employed there continue to build their own human capital by interacting with top-notch colleagues and students. Additionally, schools in geographically desirable locations may be able to pay less than schools in undesirable locations. However, when housing costs or "quality-of-life" variables are factored in, areas such as Boston, New York, Los Angeles, or San Franciso may have to pay more to bring faculty to their schools.

In recent years, public universities, which educate an increasing number of our college students, are experiencing greater difficulty competing with private schools for faculty. Given the current recession and state budget deficits, public institutions are handicapped by the strict salary schedules and limited funding imposed on them by state legislatures. Private schools on the other hand may have more freedom and flexibility to meet the market-driven demands of faculty, particularly of academic "stars." *Academe,* in its "Annual Report on the Economic Status of the Profession, 1989–90," noted that for the past several years salary increases at all private colleges and universities have been significantly higher than at all public schools.

In 1990, for example, faculty in all public schools received on average a 6.0 percent salary increase versus the 6.8 percent average increase received by all private school faculties.

However, when we disaggregate the salary statistics, we find several paradoxes. The Pacific region, where the preponderance of institutions are public including a large two-year college sector, has the highest overall salary level. Yet among the subset of elite research universities (both public and private), New England pays the highest salaries. Apparently, the typical, and less distinguished, professor on the West Coast gets paid more (e.g., $44,170 vs $34,500 on the East Coast for two-year college faculty). Yet faculty at the very best universities would get paid more if they were in New England than if they were on the West Coast ($53,380 vs $52,430 on the West Coast) (American Association of University Professors 1990). It seems that competition for prestige among elite universities in the East causes them to outbid their Western counterparts; or that competition with their nearby peer institutions forces salaries upward. In fact, in 1990 faculty at public doctoral granting research institutions received only a 5.9 percent increase, versus the 7 percent increase received by their private school counterparts (American Association of University Professors 1990). At least on the West Coast, state legislatures are putting pressure on state systems of higher education to build their two- and four-year teaching institutions, ultimately at the expense of the flagship research universities (e.g., Berkeley and UCLA in California). The influence of public agencies on the elite privates in the East is less, and so these institutions can still put the bulk of their faculty resources into hiring "stars."

THREE DIMENSIONS TO HIRING COSTS

We have divided various types of hiring costs into three categories. First, there are the resource costs to the hiring institution that accrue to the benefit of the individual being recruited. Next are the resource costs to the institution that must be considered a part of the "cost of doing business," as well as the costs to the institution associated with organizational disruption that may be caused by current labor market conditions. Finally are the costs to institutions other than the one initiating the hiring. Each of these costs will be discussed in turn.

COSTS TO THE INSTITUTION
THAT ACCRUE TO THE INDIVIDUAL

In general, costs that accrue to the individual being recruited are fairly standard, although there have been some new elements added in recent years. First, there is the cost of salary and benefits. When viewed over a professional life span of twenty to thirty years, salaries in real dollars have declined. While the period between 1960–61 and 1970–71 saw faculty salaries rise by 23 percent overall, during the next fourteen years between 1970–71 and 1983–84 faculty salaries decreased by 18.7 percent in real dollars (Bowen and Sosa 1989). The *Wall Street Journal* of April 2, 1991, reported that college professor pay increases for the current academic year failed to beat inflation for the first time in a decade, but given the large drops experienced during the 1970s, AAUP reports that real pay for faculty is still about 8 percent behind its level of twenty years ago. Ultimately, what these figures indicate is that the salary cost to institutions of hiring faculty is not rising in real dollars (any faster than the rate of inflation).

The fact that college costs are dramatically escalating while salaries remain fairly constant appears at first glance to be a contradiction. But a nine-month salary is not the only compensation that university professors receive. One way of making a given salary worth more is to reduce the teaching load. This reduces the amount of specific time a professor is obligated to spend at the university, since time spent on research or service is generally more flexible. Reduced teaching loads allow faculty to earn more on the outside, whether or not there is official sanction of such activity by the university. In order to attract top faculty, many institutions today offer reduced teaching loads, at least for the first few years, as part of a recruitment package. If there are a given number of courses to be taught, the result is that the courses not taught by the newly hired professor must be taught by lecturers or other faculty, and that will add costs to the program.

In addition, laboratory or equipment set-up costs often are part of the package for a new faculty hire. In the humanities and some social science fields these can be minimal, but in some scientific disciplines they can reach into the tens or hundreds of thousands of dollars. For universities to remain competitive, they must be able to offer top scientists the space and equipment needed to conduct their research.

Also, most college and university professors are eligible for extra compensation in addition to their nine-month teaching salary. To attract high quality faculty, extra incentives may be provided that pay for such things as computers and research assistants' time and summer employment. Additionally, moving and housing allowances are typically added in to the first year's compensation package. It is the cost of these extras that may be accounting for higher faculty compensation costs.

By way of illustration, one of the authors compared the salary and benefits he received in 1967 as a beginning assistant professor in economics (at a large midwestern university) with what he, as a dean of a School of Education (at a large West Coast university), negotiated to pay an incoming assistant professor of education in 1990. In 1967, a year in which there was high demand for faculty, the compensation for an assistant professor of economics was comprised of: $10,000 for nine months of salary, summer stipends for two summers for a total of $4,000, and a $3,000 moving allowance. Total compensation was $17,000 (or $63,623 in constant 1991 dollars). In 1990, the compensation for an assistant professor of education was comprised of: $35,000 for nine months, summer stipends for two summer months costing $7,778, a half-time research assistant for two years costing $22,132, a housing allowance of $25,000, a computer at $3,000, and a $10,000 moving allowance. Total compensation was $102,910. While the 1991 assistant professor's total compensation is greater, even in constant dollar terms, the difference is not because of variation in the regular, nine-month salary. In constant 1991 dollars, the 1967 assistant professor's salary equaled $37,425, or $2,425 more than our professor in 1991. Where the difference occurs is in the extras.

Real salaries are not increasing, but other costs are skyrocketing. The reasons for this have as much to do with the culture of the university as they do with the budget. First, despite the "salary compression" that has been discussed, there is still a sense that it is important to maintain a salary schedule. Colleagues often feel better if they know that salary level is a function of length of service, rank, and contribution to the school or department, rather than being dependent on demand and supply in the market for new hires. Thus, to the extent that nine-month salaries can be relatively standard, everyone will be happier. However, variations to allow for differing market conditions can be achieved by manipulating perks other than the basic salary.

Additionally, university culture dictates that all knowledge is equally valuable, even though market conditions work against such beliefs. Hence, there may be some incremental salary schedule for faculty in the business, medical or engineering school, but certainly not enough of a difference to compensate for the higher opportunity costs faculty in these fields encounter. Once again the perks can compensate.

Finally, faculty often vote on the level at which professors are to be hired, particularly at public institutions. In some places, the level (or step) dictates a salary as well. Deans can then provide the additional compensation to make the offer competitive. Schools want to buy prestige and they need to fill positions in a competitive market, while not breaking the salary scale. To do this, "salary" may remain relatively close to the published scale, but other compensation, such as summer salaries and housing allowances, is provided to reflect competitive bids, particularly from institutions with more flexible salary schedules. The system is not unlike the process of providing signing bonuses to star players in professional sports.

There is also a new set of costs associated with hiring faculty that has come to the fore only in the last ten years or so. More and more frequently, in order to recruit faculty, institutions need to consider the spouse. In recent years, the number of dual career families has increased dramatically. There are more women in graduate school and consequently there are more "academic marriages." Given the market conditions, the competition for faculty gives candidates more leverage to set conditions for employment, including employment for the spouse. At minimum, this may entail assisting in a job search, and at maximum it may require finding a faculty position for the spouse.

When an institution chooses to hire a desirable candidate's spouse, there are several levels of costs that may be incurred depending upon the spouse and the availability of a position. Ideally, there would be an opening and the spouse would be the best person for the position. In such a lucky but probably unusual circumstance, no additional costs should be attributed to hiring the first faculty member when his or her spouse is hired. However, a more likely scenario is one in which the spouse is not the very best candidate for an opening, but nevertheless acceptable, in which case there are only the opportunity costs of not hiring the better person. In the worst case there isn't an opening, but one is created to accommodate the sought-after candidate and his or her spouse. In such a circumstance, the opportunity costs are the full cost of hiring the spouse, and perhaps the foregone alternative of using the faculty position for a "more useful" faculty member, as well as the institutional disruption costs associated with poor morale when a suboptimally qualified person is hired.

Even when the spouse of a sought-after faculty member does not work in academe, universities are taking more responsibility for finding the spouse a job. Some institutions have established administrative offices to provide this service. Links are being built to board members, donors, and governmental agencies, so that spouses' résumés will get a quick review and preferential consideration when job openings occur in their firms or organizations.

Finally, colleges and universities increasingly are developing and funding housing assistance programs. For schools located in expensive metropolitan areas such as Los Angeles and New York, the availability of a housing assistance program can mean the difference between being competitive or not when hiring.

The University of California at Los Angeles is a prime example of this problem. When surveyed, new faculty members identified "three issues that were most important to them during their recruitment and immediately after their appointment to UCLA." "The top three issues were Affordability of Housing in Los Angeles, Locating Permanent Housing to Buy, and Choosing a Neighborhood to Live In" (Sundstrom 1990). These concerns are reasonable given that the average cost of housing within five miles of the UCLA campus is between $500,000 and $700,000 (Mangan 1988). In such a housing market, it is simply not possible for even the most well-compensated junior professor to purchase a home. Even senior recruits, unless they are moving from an equally expensive real estate market, are unable to afford housing near the campus or at least housing at all equivalent to what they must give up.

Faculty who live far from the campus tend to be less accessible, they tend to participate less in campus affairs and activities, and the quality of campus life and the important sense of academic community are put in jeopardy. To offset these problems, schools like UCLA develop extensive housing services. For example, UCLA sponsors and subsidizes a variety of housing programs. First is the Temporary Rental Housing Services, which include university-owned apartments, a guest house, and a Community Housing Office, which provides rental housing information and faculty rental coordination services. There is also a UCLA Faculty Mortgage Program, which provides real estate counseling (e.g., assistance with location/neighborhood, price range/affordability, and buy/rent decisions), and mortgage loan counseling, which provides information regarding qualifying requirements, rates and types of loans, and loan procedures. Finally, there are actual housing programs, such as the University Mortgage Assistance Program, which offer lower loan rates than might be possible if the faculty member went through a bank or mortgage company, and the University For-Sale Housing Program, which sells housing constructed or purchased by the university to selected faculty at below-market prices (Sundstrom 1990). Departmental administrators—deans and chairs—identified these services as essential in their recruiting efforts.

THE COSTS OF DOING BUSINESS: ORGANIZATIONAL DISRUPTION

For any organization there are administrative costs associated with hiring. These costs comprise the money spent advertising for, interviewing, and selecting a new person. These days, some universities are even using "head-hunter" firms that can charge several months of the recruited person's salary for their services. However, colleges and universities have special costs associated with hiring. While administrators (deans and chairs) play important roles in the academic hiring process, in peer-governed organizations like universities, faculty play a major role in recruiting and hiring future colleagues. Indeed, one of the most important and necessary processes in which faculty members engage is hiring. Good colleagues are an essential element of any college or university. But technically the time faculty spends on recruiting is in addition to the main functions of teaching, research, and service that are their official responsibilities. Thus, whenever faculty members are engaged in the hiring process, which can be quite labor- and time-intensive, there are opportunity costs. They are not teaching, conducting research, or participating in community service, and that time is in some sense lost.

Current labor market conditions may mean that highly qualified and sought-after faculty are able to command higher salaries than what people of the same rank and accomplishments already on staff are receiving. This can, and usually does, cause discontent among existing faculty, and may lead to additional costs. Typically these additional costs are of two types. Direct expenditure of additional funds will be made if schools increase salaries across the board to keep pace with escalating salaries for those recently hired. The result is that either the total budget increases or funds are diverted from other expenditure categories. On equity grounds, schools may also provide other perks such as increased research and office space, or additional research or teaching assistants to faculty already on staff, and such actions have the same effect on budgets as raising salaries.

The second set of costs consists of indirect expenses associated with poor morale that may occur when faculty seek positions elsewhere in order to have their compensation increased at their present institution by presenting a competing offer. However, when faculty members "go on the market," they may end up receiving an offer they cannot refuse, and so leave their institution to take a position elsewhere. In this case, an unanticipated opening may occur and all the costs of hiring yet another professor are incurred again.

COSTS TO OTHER INSTITUTIONS

When there is a shortage of faculty, one of the results is competition among schools for the most highly qualified people. This competition often leads to a kind of "raiding" of academic personnel and will result in higher personnel costs for both the school doing the raiding and the school being raided. Schools seeking to hire a "star" from another institution will offer everything from higher salaries, increased benefits, and more desirable working conditions to mortgage assistance and guaranteed slots for faculty member children in selective elementary schools. (Indeed, at UCLA one unmarried candidate requested assurance that if he later married and had children, these as yet unborn and unimagined children would be guaranteed a place in the University Elementary School. Despite the provost's attempt to satisfy his request, the chancellor and the dean of the Graduate School of Education decided to table it.)

Such offers cause the faculty member to either leave or become a retention case at his or her current school. If the person becomes a successful retention case, he or she is able to command a higher salary than otherwise might have been possible, and this drives up the cost of salaries at the home institution. On the other hand, if the person is hired away from the home institution, that institution will have to begin the costly process of recruitment, interviewing, and selection.

CONCLUSION

This paper has attempted to take a broad look at the wide range of costs involved when universities hire faculty members. In situations where there is a "buyer's market," that is, when the number of acceptable candidates far exceeds the number of openings, the hiring process is quite simple. In such cases, simple economics tells us that salaries should fall, and that there would be no need to "sweeten the pot" with perks to attract desirable candidates. For the most part, that was the situation from the end of the 1960s to the mid-1980s. After colleges and universities staffed up to meet peak demands as baby boomers entered college in the 1960s, enrollments leveled off, retirements were few, and there was little demand for new faculty. Even though annual production of new doctorates declined significantly, supply exceeded demand by wide margins. Although salaries rarely fall in nominal terms, the failure of academic salaries to keep pace with inflation meant that real salaries declined overall.

However, even when the academic job market was bleakest, there were situations where certain categories of faculty were in short supply. During periods of economic boom, certain industries sought engineers and scientists at the bachelor's and master's levels, and offered salaries that were high enough to discourage young graduates from pursuing the doctorate. When enrollments, particularly undergraduate enrollments, rose in fields that industry coveted, and when sitting faculty were lured to the private sector, shortages appeared in science and, more often, engineering, despite the overall depressed market. Similarly, the shortage of business school faculty, particularly in fields like finance, became legend during the heyday of the boom on Wall Street in the 1980s.

There were other instances of shortages as well. As affirmative action gained momentum, demand for nonwhite professors, and females in some fields, far outpaced the supply of them. Moreover, even in the worst of times, the top students from the very best doctoral programs, as well as "stars" already well established in academe, always have more offers than they can handle.

By the end of the 1980s, market conditions were beginning to change, as faculty hired thirty years earlier began to retire, children of the baby boomers reached college age, and the production of new Ph.D.s continued at recent low rates. Furthermore, as universities started to anticipate that shortages would occur in the mid-1990s, some began to hire before these expected shortages materialized in order to get a jump on the competition.

At this time, shortages have already become apparent: for faculty in certain fields, for certain ethnic faculty and women, for those most accomplished, and even for faculty more generally. Again, simple economics tells us how salary schedules should change; they should be increasing by amounts not seen for decades. But universities are being battered by charges that they have perpetuated uncontrollable cost spirals. Faculty are perceived by the general public as not working very hard, certainly not as hard as teachers in the public schools. Faculty are often blamed for many of society's failures, including the dismal state of public schools. And the middle class cannot afford the tuition bills at private schools that now can run to $25,000 if living expenses are factored in.

Thus, just when market conditions suggest that faculty salaries should be rising substantially, academic employers find themselves under great pressure to reduce costs. Average faculty salary levels are easily publicized—we have quoted some of them above. To the typical working voter, who fears unemployment and sees his own salary growth slowing, it is hard to tolerate the fact that a midlevel full professor at, say, UCLA earns $68,000 for nine months' work, during which time he or she is required to spend four or eight hours a week in the classroom. Hence, the chances of faculty salaries rising as much as market conditions might suggest are probably quite small.

As a result, academic employers are finding ways to attract faculty other than by paying them greatly enhanced salaries. We begin to see greater emphasis on the perks that were described earlier. Moreover, although academia has always been a very mobile profession, the need for mobility has been enhanced in recent years. The increases in demand for faculty have not been uniform across the country. Where population growth and economic booms have occurred (i.e., the Sun Belt), demand is much greater than it is in the old Rust Belt. Yet many of our best institutions of higher education remain in what may be thought of as declining regions. As departments who want to hire try to attract faculty from other regions, pressure in salaries and perks intensifies. And faculty who move want to be "made whole." That is, they want to maintain the same quality of life (e.g., residential square footage and commuting distance) and quality of work (e.g., laboratories). Thus, the perks described above become even more important.

Hiring should be a simple process. But specific faculty shortages now and impending more general shortages in the future, pressures to keep salaries down, and the need to recruit faculty from across the country who insist on duplicating their total lifestyle in their new location make hiring as much an art as a business decision.

REFERENCES

American Association of University Professors. 1990. "Some Dynamic Aspects of Academic Careers: The Urgent Need to Match Aspiration with Compensation." *Academe* (March–April): 3–29.

Blum, D. 1989. "Professors of Engineering Continue to Earn the Highest Average Salaries." *The Chronicle of Higher Education* (May 24): A14.

Bowen, W. G., and J. A. Sosa. 1989. *Prospects for Faculty in the Arts and Sciences*. Princeton, N.J.: Princeton University Press.

"College Faculty Salaries Rise Less Than Inflation." 1991. *The Wall Street Journal* (April 2): B10.

"Colleges Worry that Newly Hired Professors Earn Higher Salaries than Faculty Veterans." 1989. *The Chronicle of Higher Education* (October 18): A1–21.

Conrad, C. F., and D. J. Eagan. 1989. "The Prestige Game in American Higher Education." *The NEA Higher Education Journal* 5 (1): 5–15.

Fiske, E. B. 1989. "Shortage Predicted for '90s in Professors of Humanities." *The New York Times* (September 13): A1.

Mangan, K. 1989. "Colleges Discover that Winning a Top Faculty Recruit Sometimes Depends on Finding Work for the Spouse." *The Chronicle of Higher Education* (September 20): A13–14.

———. 1988. "With Real-Estate Prices Sky-High, More Colleges Offer Housing-Assistance Plans to Professors." *The Chronicle of Higher Education* (September 14): A15.

Mooney, C. J. 1989. "Affirmative-Action Goals Coupled with Tiny Number of Minority Ph.D.s. Set Off Faculty Recruiting Frenzy." *The Chronicle of Higher Education* (August 2): A11–12.

National Center for Educational Statistics. 1989. *Digest of Educational Statistics. 1989* (NCSE 89–643). Washington, D.C.: U.S. Government Printing Office.

Solmon, L. C., and T. L. Wingard. 1990. "The Changing Demographics: Problems and Opportunities." In *The Racial Crisis in American Higher Education*, P. G. Altbach and K. Lomotey, eds. Albany, N.Y.: State University of New York Press, pp. 19–42.

Sundstrom, P. 1990. *UCLA Faculty Housing Services Program Evaluation: Analysis of Survey Result*. UCLA Business Enterprises.

7

Working with Partners

Sue A. Blanshan and E. Gordon Gee

This chapter addresses the place of "the significant other" in the hiring processes and employment policies and practices of colleges and universities. Indeed, the significant other has become most significant with respect to an institution's ability to attract and retain ordinary, much less prime candidates for faculty and staff positions. Few colleges or universities have developed, much less perfected, the art of hiring in the context of the dual-career couple. Yet certainly their success, and for some even their survival, may depend on this very talent.

There are three fundamental points to the argument being presented and the solutions prescribed here. The first is that the spheres of work and family are not separate but deeply interwoven and integrated for both men and women. The second is that the colleges and universities of this country need the best minds to continue to

The authors wish to thank Astrid Merget and Gay Hadley for their review and comments on this chapter as it was developed. A special thank you is due to Verta Taylor for her extensive assistance in the development of the ideas presented here.

101

succeed in the development, advancement, and transmission of knowledge. Therefore, their work environments need to be receptive to all types of faculty and staff: men and women, married and single parents, live-together and commuting couples, heterosexual and gay/lesbian couples, white people and people of color, older and younger persons, etc. The third important point is that by accommodating dual-career couples in the workplace on campus, these institutions will indeed be better able to attract and keep the superior talent, among all the categories of people just mentioned, to accomplish their missions. Conversely, higher education will fail to compete for the best talent among its faculty and staff if it continues to ignore the reality and needs of dual-career couples.

An institution that designs strategies and models to help it succeed with the recruitment and retention of dual-career couples will also be more attentive to all other faculty and staff. It is the rare person who does not need to integrate work and family worlds. It is simply the dual-career couple that faces some of the most excruciating choices when this integration is ignored by the work organization.

THE MYTH

The myth of the separation of work and family has long driven our assumptions, structures, and policies in colleges and universities (Kanter 1977). The epitome of this myth is exemplified in the scientific management assumptions of the late 1940s, when academics characterized the worker (and indeed themselves by implication) as a human robot who could be programmed to carry out efficient work if one could only determine the appropriate unit of productivity (Taylor 1911). This worker had no mind, s/he had no career, no outside interests or pressures, and no relationships in or outside of work that impacted on his/her ability to perform. Today one knows that these assumptions are nonsense. Yet organizational structures, policies, and treatment of employees remain substantially based on many of these erroneous assumptions about the fragmented and segmentalized person rather than an integrated, complex person (a human being rather than a "human working").

WORK-FORCE REALITIES

In 1900 women comprised only 18 percent of the U.S. paid labor force. Forty years later women's share had risen only to about 25 percent. However, despite the baby boom, women's paid labor-force participation rose steadily after 1940. By 1985 it had risen to 44 percent of the paid U.S. labor force (Spitze 1988, p. 43). Since 1970, the greatest increases in female paid labor-force participation have been among women under age thirty-five and among mothers with preschool children (Kamerman and Kahn 1981, p. 25). As of 1987, 59 percent of all children under the age of fifteen had employed mothers (U.S. Bureau of the Census 1990). Presently half of the mothers with children under age six are working outside of the home and the incidence of dual-career families has increased, particularly in the last decade (Fox and Hesse-Biber 1984, p. 179). The number of dual-career married couples has increased from 900,000 in 1960 to 3.3 million in 1983 and now constitutes one-fifth of all working married couples. The number of dual-career families with unmarried partners is substantial in today's society. The total number of dual-career families is likely to grow at an exponential rate in the next decade (Sekaran 1986, p. 94).

In just a few short years, the growth of the work force of this country will slow down to a level not experienced since the Great Depression. The average age of the work force will rise and the availability pool of young workers entering the work force will contract. As a result of these and other trends, labor markets will be tighter. However, also by the year 2000, more women will enter the work force and an even larger number of the new entrants will be ethnic minorities. From the individual rather than the employer perspective, the slow economic growth has made two earners a necessity for many families. As the Hudson Institute points out in *Workforce 2000* (1987), the institutions and policies that govern the workplace should be reformed to allow women to participate fully in the economy and to insure that men and women have the time and resources needed to invest in their children.

THE ART OF HIRING

The art of hiring good, very good, and excellent people to work in colleges and universities is as easy and simple as any visual or performing art. That is to say, it is *not* easy and simple. Rather, the art of hiring results when some native administrative and managerial talent is combined with determination, sensitivity, hard work, trial and error, many failed attempts, an attention to detail, a global perspective, improvement with practice and more practice, a willingness to take risks, and a trust that the actual performance or final product will succeed with the "critics."

Conventional beliefs and practices can kill the art of hiring. They include the beliefs that: males are the breadwinners, women work for pin money, women and men working together will mean sex in the workplace, women should be at home with their children (Fox and Hesse-Biber 1984, p. 26), women should be in the "caring" (translates as "low-paying") professions, men have logical minds for the more precise disciplines (translates as "high-paying" positions) (Ireson and Gill 1988, pp. 142–43), women should place their male partners' careers ahead of their own (Walum 1977, pp. 143–45), women's life patterns and cycles make them less valuable to the work force (Taylor 1988, p. 176), women can have it all, women can't have it all, people who are not married do not have families that affect their work lives, and men who follow their wives' careers are failures.

Higher education will continue to practice the craft rather than the art of hiring and retaining people when it does not adequately attend to the matter of partner employment in this world of dual-career couples. It is cultural beliefs about men, women, and work rather than any specific practice that prevents one from becoming the accomplished artist that one can be, that one needs to be. Dual-career couples offer colleges and universities and their communities tremendous opportunities and talents. Minds must be open to the creative options for institutional policies and practices that could be employed if one considers dual-career people *every* time a search process is begun.

This chapter will explore the issue and dilemmas faced by dual-career couples and the problems that failure to accommodate dual-career couples cause our institutions. Next, it will look at a variety of strategies and organizational models that can help colleges and universities address the needs of dual-career couples and the organizations for which they work. Finally, the pertinent policies and policy changes for making our institutions "dual-career couple friendly" will be discussed. It is proposed that the integration of the work and family spheres is a reality, and that work structures and policies must address this reality rather than continue to be based on the myth of their separation.

INDIVIDUAL ISSUES

The issues faced by the women and men who are in dual-career partnerships are substantial. Although this type of worker has been present in the academic workplace for many decades, they have been ignored, and continue to be ignored, in spite of their increasing numbers, their dual-career difficulties, and the problems this avoidance causes colleges and universities. To understand what must be done to address the situation in a proactive manner, it is important for the reader to understand and appreciate the difficulties faced from the perspective of dual-career workers themselves. For purposes of this discussion the focus will be on issues of resources, productivity, quality of life, and identity.

MYTHS OF THE PAST

The needs of dual-career couples can in part be reviewed in the context of resources, including support systems. Two full-time careers do not allow time nor do they generally produce the income to adequately handle the care of children, older relatives, or ill family members. The care of family members is a substantial problem for working people. Although reality denies it, there is still the insidious assumption that there is someone at home to care for younger, older, and/or ill family members. The stress, guilt, crises, lost productivity, and hard choices caused due to inadequate dependent care resources represent constant problems for dual-career couples.

In reviewing the transcript of a recent panel discussion by dual-career couples (W. Arthur Cullman Symposium 1990), one is struck by the importance of having the resources to purchase services that full-time homemakers and "weekend husbands" *[sic]* have traditionally done. For women this "second shift" work amounts to a commitment of an extra month per year greater than that of their partner's if not hired out (Hochschild 1989, p.10). For example, meals are served by restaurants; laundry and cleaning is picked up and delivered by the company that does the work; children are cared for by childcare facilities, schools, and after school programs; personal conversations between partners occur on car telephones rather than in person during the evenings; lawn-care services are contracted; home cleaning is done by hired help; and pet care is attended to by small businesses set up for this purpose. It should not take long to figure out that the panel members were affluent couples able to afford the considerable expense of these services. While the average dual-career faculty member or university administrator has all of these living needs, it is the rare salary in higher education that provides the financial resources to pay for such services.

NEW REALITIES

The commuter couple is stretched even more over resource issues. Often two residences are necessary, while the expense of frequent air travel and/or automobile trips to spend some time together and substantial long-distance telephone bills all become a part of the financial stressors and hard choices. As a result, many dual-career couples can stay committed to their two careers only by making substantial financial sacrifices.

Beyond these resource issues, individuals who embrace a career do so, in part, because their involvement in it provides some meaning to their lives (Gross 1983). Therefore, their performance and productivity within their careers are important sources of satisfaction. However, the pressures and distractions of family, social, and professional life can collide, resulting in a person's performance falling below the level of her or his own expectations. That is, role overload may exact a defeating toll on the partners in dual-career relationships when their support systems are inadequate.

Particularly for women, the dilemma of role cycling—the dilemma a woman faces when she wants to have a family and a career—creates substantial performance issues. There is conflict between a woman's reproductive/parenting life cycle and her career life cycle. Both reach their peak demands at about the same time for women (Wilkie 1988, pp. 156–58). There is confusion about when to start a family and how much, if any, time may safely be taken off from one's career for raising a family without hurting her career, without losing currency in the field, without creating a gap in a résumé, and without being stigmatized by professional peers. The subjective assessments of others are, unfortunately, all too often influenced by conscious and unconscious judgments on the steady state of one's productivity from the inception of the career, and/or about the life stage during which one began a career.

These productivity factors are particularly relevant when dual-career partners consider which one of them could work part-time, accept a temporary job in transition, take a parental leave of absence to care for a young child, or take a leave of absence to care for an ill partner or other family member (Fox and Hesse-Biber 1984, pp. 192–94). Decisions of this nature are extremely stressful because all too often professional colleagues believe that they create "lost time" in a person's career that results in a stigma to be overcome (or never overcome).

VOICES IN THE WINGS

Dual-career couples also face difficult quality-of-life issues. When their careers are in the same field, they may face nepotism policies or attitudes that present barriers to their mutual employment in one unit or organization. Although higher education today generally restricts its nepotism policies to reporting lines (one's partner may not directly supervise nor determine work conditions or salary for the other), attitudes about nepotism persist among professional peers that may restrict options and quality of life. Peers may be suspicious of the couple out of a fear that confidences will not be protected, that together they have an unfair advantage through combined skills and information, or that one of them is not truly qualified for the position and only obtained it because of the influence of the partner.

Peer competition and conflict can be very stressful. However, some dual-career couples are also burdened by competition and conflict between themselves. The question of whose career comes first when there is a family crisis is not always easily resolved. One partner's promotion or recognition may not always be celebrated at home, especially if the other partner believes she or he was deserving of the same rewards and did not receive them. While work synergy is one of the advantages of working in the same field or department, sharing work without setting any boundaries on the work may mean that work consumes one's life, and there is little or no time left for relaxation or recreation.

A final quality-of-life issue for these couples can occur when there are significant social network voids. After attending to career and family responsibilities, there may be little or no time for a social life. Additionally, couples in the same field or department do not benefit from the automatic expansion of their social network as do couples in separate fields or departments.

Identity issues join the resource, productivity, and quality-of-life issues to challenge people in dual-career relationships. The myth of family and career as separate worlds is founded on the belief in gender role stereotypes that embody traditional norms of behavior. For a woman, the traditional gender role specifies that she have the children, care for them, take on the responsibility of homemaking, and subordinate her career ambitions to those of her partner. For a man, the traditional gender role specifies that he concentrate on his career success, be the head of the household, and be the principal breadwinner. Tremendous role conflict occurs for any individual in this society who behaves in a manner contrary to these proscriptions. Additionally, there are often sanctions from colleagues if one steps out of the traditonal roles. A man may be ridiculed as "spineless" if he takes on child care while a woman may be blamed for not being a good mother or homemaker, treated with contempt, or ignored in social situations with professional colleagues.

When traditionally imposed values are in opposition to one's actual behavior, stress occurs. For individuals who possess a strong internal locus of control, this stress is minimized (e.g., a woman who feels a sense of accomplishment because she has written about new discoveries in her research, and ignores gossip that she neglects her family). However, for individuals who have a strong external locus of control, the stress is maximized (Sekaran 1986, p. 39). For example, a woman who has written and published a research article in a major journal feels great until she hears gossip about having neglected her family. Then she feels worthless and a failure with both her family and career. One's self-esteem may be damaged by internal conflict about traditional versus dual-career roles or by the negative reactions of one's peers to the manner in which one responds to work or home demands.

INSTITUTIONAL ISSUES

The many dilemmas and issues faced by people in dual-career relationships are created in large part because the institutions around them do not reflect the reality of their lives. In addition to the toll exacted from the individuals, the organizations that fail to support a greater integration of work and family life also harm themselves and will continue to do so until they confront the difficult issues that must be resolved.

PAYING THE PRICE

Today there is an ever-increasing concern about the inadequacy of resources for higher education to draw from in successfully carrying out its teaching, research, and service missions. Therefore, the issue of lost institutional resources or their inefficient use must be considered. A failure to attend to adaptations for dual-career couples can further drain important resources from institutions. Inflexible work schedules and unavailable family-care resources can and often do result in high levels of absenteeism, employee inaccessibility, and turnover of staff and faculty (Fox and Hesse-Biber 1984, pp. 183–86).

The ability to retain two positions that are satisfying and appropriate for the respective careers often determines whether or not a couple will remain in a community. It is a drain on an organization's resources if, after orienting and investing time and energy in people, it loses them because they must relocate so that a partner can also be satisfactorily employed. Additionally, the potential for stress disorders that result in healthcare benefit expenses is increased if the dual-career couple is not adequately accommodated or employed.

Lost or lowered productivity of an individual or a class of individuals translates into a drop in productivity for the organization as well. Certainly in administrative work, collaboration is essential. While teamwork can in part compensate for the absence or distraction of one member, this occurs at the expense of the balance created when all members of the team are able to give a project or program their full attention. Collaborative and interdisciplinary work within dual-career couples can be a tremendous resource for colleges and universities. However, a forced separation of partners in the work setting due to nepotism attitudes can significantly harm a scholar's, and thus the institution's, research program.

PLAYING FAIR

A companion to the issue of organizational efficiency is the institutional issue of accurate system feedback. This issue is experienced by the individual as job evaluation. The assessment and evaluation of a person's performance are believed to be based on a meritocracy in higher education. However, a number of subjective factors routinely enter into performance appraisals. In the case of dual-career couples who work together, assumptions are often made that the male is the "real" author of collaborative work. When the time comes for annual performance, tenure, and promotion reviews, differential feedback that results from subjective versus merit-based criteria can serve to undercut the future motivation and productivity of a scholar (Acker 1987). Fairness on the part of evaluators, i.e., assessments based on fact rather than erroneous perceptions, is essential if organizations are to succeed in providing maximum assistance and thus obtain maximum productivity from dual-career partners.

Legal issues are present for institutions at all employment stages: recruitment, hiring, retention, and termination. Individuals have a legal right to decide whether or not they will reveal in the interview process that they are in a relationship, much less a dual-career relationship. It is illegal, as determined by federal court and EEOC decisions, to ask one about marital status, and in bad taste to ask about a candidate's personal life. However, if a candidate asks about resources for a partner's career, it is appropriate for the hiring organization to provide this information and even assistance.

Conditions and terms of employment, including salary, need to be negotiated in the context of the individual's career needs and credentials, and the institution's resources and options. The fact that a candidate's partner may also be working and/or hired by the same organization should in no way impact on the salary being offered to that person. Should a woman be paid less than comparable males in her position because her partner "was getting such a nice salary," this would be discrimination and a violation of the Equal Pay Act of 1963 (Fox and Hesse-Biber 1984, pp. 211–12). If other conditions of employment, such as the size of one's research laboratory, are affected because one is considered a "captive audience" for employment due to a partner's career commitment in this location, questions of fairness and even questions of discrimination may be raised.

Dual-career partner support programs and policies of an institution can exacerbate problems in the area of affirmative action. Given that laws and most institutional policies do not recognize partners as the hiring unit, placement of a recruit's partner should not negate affirmative-action hiring procedures (Burgan et al. 1991, p. 41). Since many dual-career policies and programs are all too often based on outdated concepts of sexual division of labor in the family, they can also negate real dual-career couple support. Yet, there is still much that can be done to support a relocating dual-career couple, without violating affirmative-action principles or imposing rigid ideas about the sexual division of labor. A respect for the rights of the individual in employment does not have to translate into a neglect of the whole person who is also part of a family unit.

All of these institutional issues can be factors that impact on the work environment. A negative environment can function as a breeding ground for significant problems like staff or faculty dissatisfaction, alienation, lost loyalty, low morale, conflict, and burnout. All of these become institutional issues rather than individual issues when the work setting is contributing to their occurrence. Organizations are often structured around certain types of gender and family roles that no longer prevail. When this happens, they become patterns of employee response rather than isolated incidents, and a drain on every type of institutional resource can be noted. A university's ability to recruit talent in the future will be diminished by the negative experience of currently and unhappily employed dual-career couples.

STRATEGIES AND MODELS

Given the reality that the spheres of work and family are not separate but rather that they explicitly and implicitly impinge on each other, institutions would be more creative and productive places if they were more responsive to the employee as a whole person. The great art of colleges and universities comes in many different forms and through many different media. However, the most fundamental ingredients for success are the talented people that one is able to hire and retain because they are satisfied with their working conditions, quality of life, and ability to be productive in a particular setting. Therefore, this section will cover some strategies and models for greater accommodation of dual-career couples. In particular, it will focus on recruitment strategies, work-pattern alternatives, potential employee resources, training mechanisms, and planning strategies for enhancing the institution's response to dual-career people.

LAYING THE MYTHS ASIDE

Recruitment can begin with statements in position advertisements that dual-career couples are acceptable or that the institution has facilitating structures for two-career family members. Such an explicit statement sends a clear and positive signal to potential candidates who may otherwise ignore the opportunity, given a partner's career needs. It is also important that the interview or selection committee include individuals who are part of dual-career couples. Such members can help to sensitize other committee members to the issues faced by dual-career couples, and can serve as both resources and role models for dual-career candidates. In cases where the candidate has indicated that (s)he has a partner who also has a career, both partners should have an opportunity in the interview process to informally raise their questions and obtain information relevant for the other's career (Burgan et al. 1991, p. 45). Taking both partners out for a meal can be a relaxing way to arrange this conversation.

For the majority of people who work in colleges and universities, the traditional eight-to-five workday is a myth. They often come to work earlier and go home later, work in the evenings, work over the weekends, and work through the "summer vacation." Indeed, some of the worst workaholics are found in higher education institutions. Students attend classes for thirteen hours throughout each day, and faculty are there to teach them; research laboratories must be monitored twenty-four hours a day, and researchers are on call if a problem arises; advisees have academic and family crises and come to their advisors for solutions at all hours of the day and night; colleagues need help to meet publication deadlines, and one reads and edits their papers on short notice; children contract contagious diseases and parents work in their home studies for two days rather than at university offices. The list goes on. While only the last example is particularly endemic to dual-career couples, the others help to demonstrate to the university the need for flexibility.

Alternative work patterns have been and will continue to be a necessity. Therefore, it would serve these institutions well if they were organized about these alternatives and had systematic knowledge of what is available and who is working under what arrangement. Flex-time and flex-place are two of the more commonly discussed options. At the time of this writing, for example, one of the authors is sitting in a home study (flex-place) writing on a laptop computer (provided by the office) on a Saturday evening (flex-time). One's productivity, not one's visibility, is the appropriate performance measure in such instances.

Alternative work patterns need to be further expanded into alternative career patterns that are endorsed as fully acceptable for professional people. All too routinely, part-time work is assumed to indicate that a person is not serious about work or career (Pearce 1987). What about tenure after a combination of years in which one has worked full-time and part-time? Career interruptions for family-care needs should not indicate career terminations. Taking a temporary position following relocation for a partner's career is often interpreted as "giving up" a career. These automatic and traumatic assumptions and conclusions must not be made. There is no good reason why part-time work can not be fully legitimated and people's professional growth in this context can not be acknowledged. Similarly, the stigma often associated with transitional and temporary positions has no useful purpose, is most often unfounded, and unnecessarily harms talented people.

Work-pattern flexibility can also be structured through the development of multiple career ladders. Not everyone with a career is well served by a vertical career ladder. Alternatives could be developed and legitimated to provide for horizontal, down, and "do not disturb" career ladders. Alternatives need to be options that are available and chosen by the individuals because they see a good fit between the alternatives, their career needs, their personality, and their family needs.

THE HELPING HAND

The organization and availability of employee resources can make a significant positive difference for dual-career partners (Fox and Hesse-Biber 1984, pp. 188–94). Compensation and benefit schemes need to be looked at and revised so that they support a positive attitude toward alternative work patterns and dual-career couples. For example, benefits need to be offered in a menu arrangement so that individuals can select the benefits they most need up to a specified value. Child care may be a high priority for some while educational benefits may be more important to others. A medical consortia for sick children with minor ailments may be a priority for people with young children. Rather than benefits to full-time employees only, an institution must consider prorating benefits for less than full-time employees (Hewitt Associates 1991). This would help eliminate some of the stigma and economic hardship of part-time work. Salary levels could be determined by skills and expertise required without being undercut by the temporary nature of a position.

Employee assistance programs provide an important set of support resources for dual-career couples. In particular, when stress disorders begin to appear, counseling services can help a great deal. Career and professional development programs that specifically take into account the needs of dual-career partners are essential resources for institutions to provide. The provision of career counseling, relocation assistance, placement services, etc., is one of the most cost-efficient resources we can offer. The provision of these services may be acquired via a contractual arrangement with other organizations or at larger colleges and universities with their own office of career and professional development for faculty and staff. The Ohio State University has an Office of Career Development for Faculty and Staff of which it is particularly proud.

A professional peer-mentoring program for dual-career partners is another valuable support resource that the institution can organize and operate. The opportunity to meet regularly with a colleague who has faced some of the same dilemmas, decisions, and career issues can provide substantial support and assistance. The increased access to information that contributes to one's success in the institution is often a direct by-product of mentoring programs.

A final institutional resource that must be provided for dual-career couples is symbolic support. Symbolic support can make visible and legitimate dual-career partners and their families. For example, the acknowledgement of the importance of dual-career couples in speeches given by the president and senior administrators of the institution lends credibility to these individuals. The organization can sponsor a "family day" during which employees and their family members picnic and play together. An award could be given annually to the Dual-Career Couple of the Year. Symbolic support should not be underestimated as organizations set about the business of affirming dual-career couples.

EDUCATE THE EDUCATORS

Planning is essential as institutions work to change into settings that recruit and retain dual-career couples with considerable ease and success. Information systems can be developed that help to monitor employee characteristics and their profiles. Such monitoring can help the institution anticipate changing needs in the benefits package, in the work-pattern options, in the recruitment to fill vacancy, etc. As work-force demographics change, one can anticipate many of the adaptations that organizations will need to make in the near future. Anticipating and planning rather than waiting for a crisis is certainly preferable.

Recent work on strategic planning and managing corporate cultures offers some useful guidance. In a very real sense, what is being prescribed is, indeed, a culture change in colleges and universities. There must be an openness to new values, roles, behaviors, work and living patterns, and dual-career couples. Benningson (1985, pp. 31–32) suggests that changing an organization's culture involves implanting new knowledge and values, developing a shared vision, determining the desired behavior, reorienting power to support new values and behavior, and harnessing the management systems that have a high impact on change processes. Sekaran (1986, pp. 156–57) offers an action plan for organizations that wish to address dual-career couple issues. She recommends that this action plan include: an audit of dual-career family members; an evaluation of policies; an assessment of child care; a review of alternate work-pattern arrangements; career pathing, training and mentoring; and counseling. Both of these authors underscore the importance of planning.

Training members in every corner of these organizations to be responsive to and affirming of dual-career partners is a final and essential strategy for making the necessary changes. Interviewers must be trained in how to signal support of dual-career candidates without violating the law. Department heads need to be coached in how to be creative with respect to creating alternative work patterns that successfully get the work done and accommodate dual-career people. Supervisors and managers must be trained to have and utilize realistic and fair performance appraisal skills. Dual-career partners should themselves have access to training that helps them develop and heighten their own sense of competence and self-esteem.

Beyond these strategies and mechanisms for changing institutions so that they will be more supportive of dual-career couples and thus more successful in hiring and retaining them, colleges and universities will need to review, change, and add policies that help to support both work and family life. This is the subject of the next section of this chapter.

POLICIES

Most current personnel policies in higher education are based on
the myth of the separation of family and work. The life-style assumptions of these policies are generally unstated but must be analyzed
in order to pave the way for change. The synthesis of policy and
practice will not only help to present a consistent posture to dual-
career partners in hiring and retention work, but it will also help
to assure that the philosophical and moral commitments institutions
make with respect to humane and fair treatment of our faculty and
staff are developed and communicated in a clear manner. It is not
enough simply to change behavior and strategies for a few particularly
desirable recruits. One must be about the business of writing the
score for the entire orchestra, i.e., developing recruitment policies,
not operating with idiosyncratic practices. Policies help to articulate
the values, principles, and resulting practices of an entire organization.
The policy areas of compensation, benefits, and the integration of
the work and family spheres are of particular relevance for dual-
career couples.

As mentioned earlier, a review and revision of benefit schemes
in the context of dual-career couples is important. Benefit policies
and programs cost institutions a tremendous amount. Therefore, they
should be designed to help obtain and retain all people needed to
accomplish their goals.

> Benefit policies that view every family member as "dependent"
> are outdated. Indeed, benefit policies that require a partner
> to be a legally married spouse are outdated and do not reflect
> the reality of today's society.

Employees' families are configured very differently today than they
were when most of our benefit programs and policies were designed.
It is time to catch up with reality.

> Benefit policies that force choices onto employees that are
> either minimally utilized or part of the benefit profile only
> because they cost so little need to be reexamined.

Institutions should seriously consider the development and
implementation of cafeterial style benefit schemes.

A basic core of benefits could be wrapped with chosen benefits
that the employees decide on up to a given dollar value. For example,
a set number of leave days, long-term disability, worker's compensation, and retirement benefits could provide the core benefits. Then
employees would be free to choose among medical care, dental care,
vision care, child-care vouchers, flexible spending accounts, education fees, and life insurance benefits.

Comparable worth has typically been associated with the comparison of salaries between positions traditionally held by women
and those traditionally held by men.

However, it is time that the concept and resulting policies
be extended to comparable worth with respect to full-time
and part-time work; with respect to permanent and temporary
appointments; and so forth.

Leave time need not be specified as sick, personal, or vacation.

Leave policies could set the number of days of leave in a year, and
then individuals could use it whether they are sick, having a baby,
adopting a baby, a child is ill, a parent has surgery, they are going
on vacation, and so forth.

In addition, leave policies need to be reviewed and opened
up to allow for paternity, maternity, adoption, major illness,
family crisis, etc., leaves.

Institutions need to develop policies and resources for family
care rather than simply child care.

Indeed, many employees spend considerable time and energy in caring for elder parents. Policymakers cannot turn their backs on this
as if the reality would disappear.

Policies on family-care leave which guarantee a return to the
job need to be considered.

A flexible work-pattern policy should specify the parameters of flex-time, flex-place, etc.

It would signal full institutional support for creative work-arrangement alternatives.

Further integration of the work and family spheres can be accomplished through policy leadership. For example, as Kanter (1977, p. 96) recommends,

a Family Responsibility Statement be issued.

Such a statement would make it clear that a given organization is guided by the principle that fundamental to all of its activities is a concern that families be supported and not disrupted by work.

All policies and operations would be subject to a "family friendly" review based on such a statement.

A relocation assistance policy would help to provide a consistent and visible support service to dual-career couples.

This type of policy, complemented by relocation and placement assistance facilities and services, is perhaps one of the most forthright signals that an institution can offer that it truly cares about dual-career partners.

Therefore, in light of dual-career needs, institutions must begin by reviewing all of their personnel policies to assess their current ability to address these needs.

This assessment would cover benefit offerings and options, salary schedules (part-and full-time), leaves of absence (length and bases), family-care services, work patterns, and institutional values/mission.

CONCLUSION

In this chapter, the issues that dual-career partners struggle with at home and in the workplace have been discussed. In addition, the problems and dilemmas faced by the organizations that hire dual-career partners without considering their needs were presented. Strategies and organizational models that can be created and utilized by institutions to be more responsive to the needs of dual-career couples were proposed. Finally, a description of some policies that will support the integration of the spheres of work and family was outlined. What has been offered in this chapter is not an exhaustive presentation of all the options available to recruit and retain dual-career couples. Rather, it should stimulate your own thinking to go beyond what has been presented here and to adapt these ideas to the particulars or your own college or university.

Dual-career couples are very much present in higher education institutions today. They will increase in the coming years (Gee 1991). These couples offer talent that institutions want and need. It is essential to respond to dual-career couples' needs for their sakes and for the sake of these institutions.

REFERENCES

Acker, Joan. 1987. "Sex Bias in Job Evaluation." In *Ingredients for Women's Employment Policy,* edited by Bose and Spitze. Albany, N.Y.: State University of New York Press.

Blau, Francine, and Marianne Ferber. 1986. *The Economics of Women, Men, and Work.* Englewood Cliffs, N.J.: Prentice-Hall.

Bruce, Willa. *Dual Career Couples in the University: Policies and Problems.* Paper presented at the annual conference of the National Association for Women Deans, Administrators, and Counselors, Nashville, Tenn., March 1990.

Burgan, Mary, George Butte, Karen Houck, and David Laurence. 1991. "Two Careers, One Relationship: An Interim Report on 'Spousal' Hiring and Retention in English Departments." In *American Departments of English Bulletin* 98: 40–45.

Fox, Mary Frank, and Sharlene Hesse-Biber. 1984. *Women at Work.* Mountain View, Calif.: Mayfield.

Friedman, Dana. 1989. *Family Supportive Policies: The Corporate Decision-Making Process.* New York: The Conference Board.

Gee, E. Gordon. 1991. "The Dual-Career Couple: A Growing Challenge." *Educational Record* (Winter 1991).

Gershuny, Jonathan, and John P. Robinson. 1988. "Historical Changes in the Household Division of Labor." *Demography* 25:537–52.

Giele, Janet Zollinger. 1988. "Gender and Sex Roles." In *Handbook of Sociology,* edited by N. Smelser. Newbury Park, Calif., pp. 291–326.

Gross, Harriet Engel. 1983. "Couples Who Live Apart: Time/Place Disjunctions and Their Consequences." In *Feminist Frontiers,* edited by Richardson and Taylor. Reading, Mass.: Addison-Wesley.

Hewitt Associates. 1991. "Survey of Benefits for Part-Time Employees." Lincolnshire, Ill.: Hewitt Associates.

Higher Education Research Institute. 1991. "The American College Teacher: National Norms for the 1989–90 I.E.R.I. Faculty Survey." Published by University of California at Los Angeles.

Hochschild, Arlie. 1989. *The Second Shift: Inside the Two-Job Marriage.* New York: Viking.

Hudson Institute. 1987. *Workforce 2000: Work and Workers for the Twenty-first Century.* Indianapolis: Hudson Institute.

Ireson, Carol, and Sandra Gill. 1988. "Girls' Socialization for Work." In *Women Working,* edited by Stromberg and Harkess. Mountain View, Calif.: Mayfield.

Kamerman, Sheila B., and Alfred Kahn. 1981. *Child Care, Family Benefits, and Working Parents: A Study in Comparative Policy.* New York: Columbia University Press.

Kanter, R. 1977. *Work and Family in the United States: A Critical Review and Agenda for Research and Policy.* New York: Sage.

Mangan, Katherine S. 1989. "Colleges Discover That Winning a Top Faculty Recruit Sometimes Depends on Finding Work for a Spouse." *Chronicle of Higher Education* 36 (3):13–14.

Parsons, Talcott. 1943. "The Kinship System in the Contemporary United States." *American Anthropologist* 45: 22–38.

Pearce, Diana M. 1987. "On the Edge: Marginal Women Workers and Employment Policy." In *Ingredients for Women's Employment Policy,* edited by Bose and Spitze. Albany, N.Y.: State University of New York Press.

Pingree, S., M. Butler, W. Paisley, and R. Hawkins. 1978. "Anti-Nepotism's Ghost: Attitudes of Administrators Toward Hiring Professional Couples." *Psychology of Women Quarterly* 3 (1): 22–29.

Preissler, Scott M. 1989. "Job-Search Help for the 'Trailing Spouse.' " *Journal of Career Planning and Employment* 50 (1): 83–84.

Reed, C. 1988. "Anti-Nepotism Rules and Dual Career Couples: Policy Questions for Public Personnel Administrators." *Public Personnel Management* 18 (1): 223–29.

Reskin, Barbara. 1991. "Labor Markets as Queues: A Structural Approach to Changing Occupational Sex Segregation." In *Macro-Micro Linkages in Sociology,* edited by J. Huber. Newbury Park, Calif.: Sage.

Sekaran, Uma. 1986. *Dual Career Families.* San Francisco: Jossey-Bass, 1986.

Smart, Mollie S., and Russell Smart. 1990. "Paired Prospects: Dual-Career Couples on Campus." *Academe,* pp. 33–37.

Spitze, Glenna. 1988. "The Data on Women's Labor Force Participation." In *Women Working,* edited by Stromberg and Harkess. Mountain View, Calif.: Mayfield.

Spitze, Glenna, and Joan Huber. 1980. "Changing Attitudes toward Women's Nonfamily Roles: 1938 to 1978." *Journal of Work and Occupations* 7:317–35.

Spitze, Glenna, and Scott South. 1985. "Women's Employment, Time Expenditure, and Divorce." *Journal of Family Issues* 6:307–30.

Stromberg, Ann Helton, and Shirley Harkess. 1988. *Women Working.* Mountain View, Calif.: Mayfield.

Summary Proceedings, The Fifth Biennial W. Arthur Cullman Symposium 1990. *Women in Leadership . . . Dawn of a New Decade.* Columbus, Ohio: The Ohio State University.

Taylor, Frederick W. 1911. *Scientific Management.* New York: Harper.

Taylor, Patricia. 1988. "Women in Organizations: Structural Factors in Women's Work Patterns." In *Women Working,* edited by Stromberg and Harkess. Mountain View, Calif.: Mayfield.

U.S. Bureau of the Census. 1989. *Statistical Abstracts of the United States.* Washington, D.C.: U.S. Government Printing Office.

———. 1990. "Who's Minding the Kids? Child Care Arrangements Winter 1986–87." *Current Population Reports,* Series P–70, no. 20. Washington, D.C.: U.S. Government Printing Office.

Walum, Laurel Richardson. 1977. *The Dynamics of Sex and Gender: A Sociological Perspective.* Chicago: Rand McNally.

Wilkie, Jane Riblett. 1988. "Marriage, Family, and Women's Employment." In *Women Working,* edited by Stromberg and Harkess. Mountain View, Calif.: Mayfield.

8

Hiring Women and Minorities

Marian J. Swoboda

RECRUITMENT AND THE INSTITUTIONAL ENVIRONMENT

Recruiting women and minorities for faculty positions in higher education requires an ongoing commitment to achieving diversity among faculty members and administrators. Recruitment must be seen as a continuous process, not a one-shot effort that begins and ends with the filling of a position. Successful recruitment depends on the attitudes and policies that shape an institution's overall working environment. Although rarely focused on by hiring committees, the working environment is one of the most important factors in the successful recruitment and retention of women and minorities. Because an unwelcoming environment can counteract the best efforts of a department chair or hiring committee, and because the working environment cannot be quickly altered as hiring needs arise, cultivating an environment attractive to women and minority applicants must be treated as a top priority.

In cultivating a supportive, inclusive environment, faculty members and administrators must recognize that diversifying the faculty means more than simply complying with federally mandated affirmative action requirements. It is in reality fundamental to the mission and the competitive position of the institution. Above and beyond the intellectual value of diverse viewpoints and the need to serve an increasingly diverse student population, as the turn of the century approaches and the current generation of senior faculty retires, colleges and universities will be hiring large numbers of new faculty from a candidate pool with a high proportion of women. The proportion of Ph.D.s granted to women in 1989–90 reached 41.5 percent, and continues to increase. Combined with the 11.9 percent of doctorates granted to minorities in the same year,* it must be noted that the applicant pool for faculty positions already comprises over half women and minorities. As hiring becomes increasingly competitive, those colleges and universities that offer the best working environments will inevitably have a larger pool of candidates from which to choose.

Success in recruiting women and minorities is a circular process. Candidates are attracted to institutions with warm, supportive working environments; campuses with such environments are not only more successful in bringing women and minorities on board, but in keeping them professionally and personally satisfied. Women and minorities happy at and committed to their institution will not only spread the word but will be available to assist actively in ongoing recruitment efforts for other women and minority faculty members.

Negative Attitudes Impede the Hiring Process

Rather than looking at the overall environment at their institution, those engaged in recruiting often focus instead on "hiring a woman" or "hiring a minority," and as a result their good intentions may be undercut by negative attitudes. Such attitudes include the assumption that minorities won't want to come because there are few of them in the community, the fear that they will expect large salaries, and the belief that no qualified minority or female candidates exist. This last belief is perhaps the most insidious and difficult to dispel; it is often invoked to veil deeply held beliefs of ethnic or gender

---

*U.S. Department of Education, National Center for Education Statistics, Integrated Postsecondary Education Data System (IPEDS), "Completions" Survey, for the academic year 1989–90. Non-resident aliens are excluded from all totals.

inferiority. Even the language often used in position announcements—"qualified women and minorities are encouraged to apply"—carries the connotation that such candidates are otherwise less qualified.

This type of negative mind-set becomes a self-fulfilling prophecy. The institution not only is likely to fail in its initial goal of hiring a woman or minority, but also works against its long-term goal of establishing an open, supportive working environment. The negative mind-set operates under the assumption that the department or institution itself is completely neutral, objective, and rational in its decision-making process, and that pervasive cultural forces of ethnic and gender bias simply do not exist. If this assumption underlies screening decisions and candidate evaluations, then there is an automatic danger that rejection of a minority or female candidate will be unequivocally construed as reflecting the candidate's lack of qualifications or interest, rather than reflecting subconscious prejudice. If the possibility of subconscious ethnic and gender bias is not admitted, then such bias will not be recognized, let alone eliminated, when it occurs.

Establish Need for Diversity

In addition to anticipating the possibility of subconscious prejudice, deans, chairs, and hiring committee members need to embed within their departments a sense of the importance of diversification in higher education. They should spell out specific programmatic reasons for adding women or minority scholars to the faculty so that the committee will feel internally motivated, rather than externally pressured, to seek diverse candidates. For example, beyond the importance of gender and cultural issues within the curriculum itself, in many fields there remains a critical need for appropriate mentors and role models for students. The members of the hiring committee must believe that diversity will enhance the department and help it achieve its academic mission, not that the department or institution is being compelled by political or social pressure to hire diverse candidates. Unfortunately, the latter is often the case. Though they might not say so aloud, committee members may feel that hiring a woman or minority is being done simply to meet affirmative action goals. Candidates who sense this feeling within a hiring committee are apt to feel patronized and fear that, if hired, they'll be ghettoized, treated as a token whose academic credentials are suspect rather than as a scholar who happens to be female or of non-European heritage.

Poor Environment Leads to Poor Recruiting Record

When an institution with a nonsupportive environment succeeds in adding a woman or minority to its faculty, affirmative action invariably ends there. The institution provides no ongoing support for the new hire because, being perfectly neutral on issues of race and gender, it does not perceive the disadvantages or unique challenges women and minority faculty members face. No acknowledgment, let alone assistance, is offered with respect to spousal placement, child-care needs, or potential hostility, harassment, or discrimination. Rather than being welcomed as an essential part of an ongoing, unified effort toward expanding the academic community as a whole, the new hire is isolated as a token; the goal having been met, special efforts toward inclusion are dropped. The new hire is left to "sink or swim." If, as often happens at nonsupportive institutions, women and minority faculty members "sink"—leave quickly, or have difficulty making tenure—this is seen as evidence that they are inherently less qualified, rather than evidence that the institutional environment is deficient.

The negative environment at such institutions is thus self-reinforcing, from the perspectives of both those involved in hiring and those considering applying. The hiring committee's initial doubts about minority and female candidates appear to be confirmed, leaving the committee members even more skeptical about "wasting their efforts" next time. And disenchanted women and minority scholars put out the word about the institution's poor environment for women and minorities, warning potential candidates away. The college acquires a reputation as a revolving-door institution lacking a genuine interest in diversity, and as a difficult place for women and minority scholars to achieve professional satisfaction.

POSITIVE ATTITUDES, SUPPORTIVE POLICIES

To break the negative cycle and achieve success in recruiting women and minorities, institutions must examine the attitudes and policies that shape the working environment. Just as negative attitudes under-mine the affirmative action process, so positive attitudes all but ensure its success. Schools and departments that embrace the conviction that diversity is a top priority and that qualified candidates do exist inevitably succeed in finding them. However, such institutions recog-nize that attracting diverse candidates requires a different approach from standard hiring practices. When female and minority candidates appraise an institution, they are looking beyond the school's physical facilities and academic reputation. They are looking for subjective qualities that indicate whether the school will advance or impede their career. No matter how eminent an institution by objective measurements, a frustrated or unhappy scholar is not likely to make professional progress.

An institution can assess the quality of its working environment in many ways. At the most basic empirical level, administrators should follow closely statistics on the numbers of women and minority faculty, within each school and department, being hired and granted tenure, and compare these figures with the percentages of women and minori-ties receiving doctorates in corresponding fields of study. However, it must be emphasized that a good record of hiring diverse faculty does not necessarily imply a supportive working environment; reten-tion and exit figures must be examined as well. An institution with poor retention rates—a "revolving door"—may wish to conduct exit interviews to discover the reasons its women and minority faculty members are leaving. Salary disparities between minority and majority groups within the institution must be gauged and eliminated. Other factors administrators can measure with some degree of objectivity include the equitability of work assignments, the rigor and fairness with which personnel procedures are articulated and enforced, and the availability of supportive services like mentoring, child care, and conflict resolution capabilities. Finally, on a more intuitive level, administrators can keep a finger on the institution's pulse by being sensitive to the social distance between majority and minority faculty members as well as the language of daily exchange on the campus. While these aspects of the working environment are admittedly more subtle and subjective, they may prove the most revealing about what the institution is like for the women and minorities who work there.

An institution's reputation will precede it, and good word-of-mouth is a priceless asset that can be developed and reinforced through networking techniques. But a college without a high profile, or one just beginning to implement an aggressive affirmative action program, will need to project warmth, sincerity, enthusiasm, flexibility, and an abiding commitment to diversity. These are qualities which must be cultivated within the institution—qualities that cannot be faked. People can detect whether others are truly comfortable working with those different from themselves; they can distinguish genuine conviction and interest from superficial compliance and "going through the motions."

Standard hiring practices let the candidates apply for a position, and then try to sell themselves to the department. If no minorities or women apply, none are hired. Successful affirmative action programs take the opposite approach: the hiring committee goes out and searches for candidates, and then assumes the responsibility of selling their department and school to the candidate. Rather than testing a candidate's interest in their institution by focusing on its shortcomings, as hiring committees are sometimes prone to do, the committee should project excitement about the department, pride in its achievements, and optimism toward its challenges. Instead of second-guessing applicants and focusing on what they themselves perceive as potential detractions, such as lack of a minority community or modest salaries, hiring committee members should focus on the attractive professional opportunities their school and department offer.

While salaries should certainly reflect the academic marketplace as a whole, institutions successfully committed to diversity have found that salary level is usually a secondary consideration. A less than grand salary will not deter a candidate attracted to the institution for other reasons; likewise, an institution can rarely overcome an unwelcoming, negative environment by a lucrative offer.

Beyond projecting an attitude of openness and commitment to diversity, successful institutions back up their positive attitudes with policies to promote a favorable working environment. These policies, addressing both academic and social concerns, are designed to overcome traditional stumbling blocks in recruiting and retaining women and minority faculty members.

Academic Factors Influence Hiring Success

On the academic front, institutions with a supportive work environment take a nurturing approach to faculty development. In contrast to the traditional "sink or swim" approach, the tenure-track period is used as an opportunity to facilitate faculty development. Two problems frequently cited by women and minorities as serious impediments to their academic progress are a lack of faculty mentors and overwhelming service requests.

The availability of appropriate mentors has been described as the most important factor in the academic development and success of new faculty members, yet many institutions have no mentoring system. Instead, they rely on informal networking within the department, which is most often based on common academic interests and male bonding. Female and minority scholars, particularly those pursuing research on gender or ethnic issues, are often isolated within departments, and thus at a great disadvantage when their work comes up for review, as well as missing out on the exchange and flow of ideas so central to academic life. Supportive institutions avoid isolating new faculty by adopting official mentoring policies. While departments need not impose specific matches between senior and junior faculty members, chairs can make certain that new members connect right away with at least one person in the department. Establishing solid mentor relationships not only helps new faculty members launch their careers, but also cultivates loyalty. And because collegiality is a major factor in retaining faculty members who receive lucrative offers from other schools, instilling a sense of loyalty and belonging should be regarded as an important institutional goal.

Institutions that have taken steps to bring women and minorities on board need to take further steps to protect them from service overload. In addition to their regular teaching and research responsibilities, minority and women faculty often face a disproportionate number of demands for nonacademic services such as extra student counseling, organizational leadership, and community outreach. New faculty members are often reluctant to refuse such requests, fearing loss of friends, support networks, and credibility, as well as a sense of betrayal of commitment. Yet to take on extended extracurricular activities may well compromise their academic work. Departments should monitor faculty caseloads and either be prepared to insulate their recent hires from excessive service requests, or else take such extra nonacademic services into account when faculty performance comes up for review. When such positive environmental changes are successfully instituted, word travels through academic networks, thereby serving to attract diversified candidates. At the same time, these very factors become potent selling points for hiring committees.

Social Policies Fulfill Special Needs

In the social arena, meeting the needs of women and minorities in higher education requires policy-setting at the institutional, rather than departmental level. Women faculty often have greater needs for assistance with spousal employment and child care, though with the increase in two-career and dual-academic couples, these issues are fast becoming a consideration for most academics. Institutions which can offer affordable, on-campus child care, flexible family leave policies, established spousal placement programs, and an overall environment of support for faculty members coping with the often conflicting demands of family and career will have a significant recruiting edge.

Women and minorities also take comfort in knowing that a campus has well-recognized complaint procedures. The existence of effective, publicized complaint procedures sends the message that the institution recognizes the possibility of discrimination and harassment; whereas colleges lacking formalized policies may be attempting to deny that such problems can, and do, occur.

Finally, hiring committees must realize that women and minority applicants will be understandably reluctant to bring up these issues during the interview process. While hiring committees should not inquire as to a candidate's family status, they should be sure that the social support services and policies offered at their institution are clearly conveyed to the candidate.

Institutions with broad-based policies designed to avert problems in such sensitive areas as mentoring, service loads, family needs, and complaint procedures—and which articulate these policies duirng the hiring process—will powerfully communicate to candidates their understanding of the particular challenges faced by women and minorities, and their commitment to an environment that will support and nurture a diverse faculty.

THE SEARCH PROCESS

A supportive environment not only helps attract a targeted candidate, but also facilitates the targeting process itself. A campus environment that supports diversity, anchored by positive attitudes and policies, is self-perpetuating: it fosters networks within the broader academic community and greatly enhances communication and interest among minorities and women in faculty openings at the institution. Such networks—which take time and energy to build and sustain—remain the single best tool for an institution in establishing credibility and locating candidates.

Develop Recruiting Networks

To cultivate effective recruiting networks, administrators and faculty members involved in hiring must become constantly aware of networking and recruiting opportunities. Recruiting and targeting potential candidates should occur not just during a formal search, but must become part of day-to-day teaching, research, and mentoring activities. As a starting point, women and minority faculty already at the institution are a rich source of recommendations and referrals. Provided that they are satisfied with the institution, such faculty members will gladly recommend names of friends, colleagues, and recent graduates who are potential candidates, and will pass the word along through this network about their school's positive environment. Beyond the faculty resources within their own departments, chairs and hiring committees can tap women and minority colleagues throughout the campus, or throughout the system in a multi-campus institution, as well as contacting colleagues at other schools through mutual friends, conferences, visiting scholar programs, and so forth. In addition to establishing all-important personal contacts, deans and chairs should acquire lists of those minorities receiving grants and fellowships to complete doctoral programs, and those presenting talks at conferences, writing or coauthoring papers, or achieving notable success in the arts or professions.

Use Innovative Recruiting Strategies

Colleges and universities should also consider specific procedural tools that have proven helpful in recruiting for diversity. Institutions need to augment the traditional method of recruiting faculty: announcing an opening through mailings and advertisements, waiting for applications to arrive and hoping a few will have the desired credentials. They need to adopt the mentality of athletic coaches and corporate executives: go out and find the talent.

Many schools and departments have formed relationships with predominantly minority colleges. Minority colleges that confer doctoral degrees offer a fertile source of new faculty and will happily guide their new Ph.D.s toward institutions with whom they have established connections and where they believe their alumni will find professional satisfaction. Many universities have relaxed their prohibitions on hiring their own Ph.D.s in order to begin cultivating potential faculty members earlier in the academic pipeline, bringing in promising graduate students and grooming them for future recruitment. Undergraduate minority and women's colleges should not be overlooked as an excellent source of future doctoral candidates.

To encourage departments to focus on results and develop aggressive recruiting campaigns, administrators can implement a variety of tried and tested incentive strategies. Target of Opportunity Programs (TOP) award new tenure-track positions to departments that identify outstanding scholars with targeted or underrepresented groups. Such programs are viewed as powerful recruiting tools because of the flexibility and rapid response time they permit. A department that spots a promising new Ph.D. can court the scholar and make the offer virtually at once—without waiting for a position to open up and without going through the protracted advertising and screening process. Sometimes TOP slots are awarded on a competitive basis to the departments presenting the best slate of candidates matching the department's needs, or to reward departments with a strong prior record of recruiting for diversity. A more experimental variant of the TOP concept involves "cluster hiring" a group of underrepresented scholars within a discipline or related fields to avoid tokenism and generate internal support networks that enhance retention and, in turn, recruitment.

Colleges and universities should also be on the lookout for women and minority scholars already established in their field who might fit a current opening. While such scholars may not be actively looking for other employment, special efforts to reach them may well be worth the added experience and prestige they have to offer. In addition, hiring at the tenure level helps avoid the retention problems many institutions experience with new Ph.D.s. who may be more easily overwhelmed or discouraged by a less-than-ideal working environment.

Other approaches that do not require establishing new-line positions but still allow institutions to grab good prospects include visiting-scholar programs and postdoctoral fellowships. In both cases, targeted scholars can be brought onto the campus in one relatively fast, smooth step, where they can then be carefully mentored and courted until a position opens up. Or promising scholars can be hired at the lecturer level with the assurances of being promoted to fill an anticipated tenure-track opening within a short time. One approach gaining popularity involves creating part-time extended tenure-track positions. A full-time position can be shared by two people in the same department, or even split to create two half-time positions in different departments. Such reduced work-load arrangements are particularly attractive to individuals with extensive family commitments.

Institutions should also support individual faculty members who make the time and commitment to diversify their departments. For example, departments can lighten the academic load of faculty involved in intensive affirmative action recruiting, and administrators can reimburse departments that give such release time to their faculty. Some institutions provide travel grants to faculty who spend extra time at conferences developing recruitment contacts, and schools should not overlook the possibility of giving additional research support to faculty bearing a heavy recruitment load or to those especially involved with mentoring diverse faculty or graduate students.

Finally, in addition to "carrot" approaches, institutions can also use "sticks" to reinforce their commitment to diversity. Administrators can impose a hiring freeze on departments whose efforts to diversify remain unsuccessful, and can redistribute faculty positions, taking them from relatively segregated departments and giving them to departments demonstrating an active pursuit of diversity in hiring.

When the Search Begins

Adopting innovative approaches to affirmative action, such as "growing your own" faculty or waiving open recruitment, does not require settling for second best. What it does require is initiative, flexibility, awareness, and effective leadership throughout the process, from the composition of the hiring committee to the courting of a targeted candidate.

The hiring committee must be able to represent diverse interests regardless of the gender and cultural background of the members. If possible the committee should be integrated, perhaps drawing on people from other departments. Some institutions make a point of including a "watchdog" on the committee, who has the added assignment of monitoring the whole search and screen process for biased or inappropriate behavior. But all members need to be genuinely comfortable with and interested in people with backgrounds and viewpoints different from their own, as well as sensitive to the ways that unconscious stereotypes can affect candidate screening and evaluations.

If the search is guided by a specific position description, the language should be as broad and inclusive as possible, both to maximize the pool of potential candidates and to permit maximum flexibility during the screening process. A narrow, rigid position description tailored to a department's immediate short-term needs may eliminate a candidate who might not have the precise qualities described, but who nevertheless complements the department well in other ways. Specifying within the description that scholars with background or teaching experience in women's or ethnic studies are particularly sought will encourage a diverse pool of applicants, including some who might not have responded to a more restricted position description.

Once the screening process is under way, the committee should keep applicants apprised of the status and completion of their applications and the anticipated timetable for reviewing submitted materials. As they begin arriving on campus, particular attention needs to be given to women and minority applicants: committee members have to anticipate and prevent awkward questions and comments that could skew the interview process, leading to inappropriate conclusions by the committee members or to discomfort on the applicant's part.

As the applicants are assessed, deans, chairs, and hiring committee members must again be sensitive to how unconscious stereotypes and fears of lowering academic standards can affect evaluations. Committee members who feel that seeking diversity means subordinating considerations of scholarship to considerations of diversity may actually demand higher achievements of women and minority applicants. So fearful are they of compromising inequality, they may be unable to look neutrally at the candidate as a scholar, let alone to regard a different background and viewpoint as a desirable quality in its own right. When the applicant is clearly a superstar, this tendency may not be a problem; but when an applicant's qualifications are more ambiguous, subtle and unconscious attitudes within the hiring committee can determine whether the applicant is viewed in the best or the worst possible light.

When credentials appear uneven or marginal, it may well be worth the committee's while to dig a little deeper to find the story behind the facts. For example, an otherwise qualified applicant may seem light on publications, but checking with colleagues in the same field of specialty might reveal that the applicant has been studying a particularly difficult problem with only recent—but highly significant—results. However, a hiring committee is unlikely to make the effort unless it feels positive about the applicant in other ways; if members harbor intrinsic doubts about the applicant, for reasons having nothing to do with the applicant's résumé, they may—without being aware of it—go out of their way to magnify, rather than downplay, the applicant's weak points. The opposite will be true for an applicant about whom committee members have a "good feeling"—the source of which may be nothing more than the applicant's similarity to themselves. It is, therefore, essential that department leaders carefully monitor the screening process and be prepared to elicit and dispel any suspicion or discomfort within the committee about seeking diversity.

When a Candidate Is Targeted

Once the search has been narrowed to a well-qualified candidate, the recruiting network can again be tapped to help court the candidate. Institutions with successful affirmative action programs have found that phone calls through the network are more effective than letters in conveying to the candidate sincerity and a personal touch. Group approaches can be particularly effective when different faculty and administrators contact the candidate periodically to represent their personal perspectives and solicit the candidate's views; a candidate who feels inhibited talking with a dean or chair might open up to another faculty member, especially another woman or ethnic minority. In addition, the more impressions gained of the candidate, the more well-rounded and thorough the final evaluation can be. While phone calls express more personal interest in the candidate than letters, all telephone contacts should be followed up with personal letters to reinforce the candidate's sense of being genuinely wanted for his or her unique qualities. The active involvement of upper-level administration such as provosts, vice-chancellors, chancellors, vice-presidents, and presidents has also proven extremely effective in communicating the depth of the institution's interest in the candidate and commitment to diversity.

Do as We Say . . . *AND* as We Do

Finally, any college or university committed to diversifying its faculty must begin by taking a good look at itself. Is its own senior-level administration integrated? Or is there a "glass ceiling" beyond which women and minorities cannot rise? An exclusively white male senior administration, no matter how well intentioned, sends a mixed message to its departments and hiring committees. A department can hardly be criticized for using the excuse that "there aren't any out there" when its own administration makes the same excuse. An institution must incorporate diversity within its own administration if it is to establish credibility among its departments and faculty members, and to impress upon them the seriousness of diversity as a mission of the institution and of academe as a whole.

9

Lessons from the Corporate World

Ronald H. Stein and Ronald Caruso

Perhaps the best-known recruiting is that which is done by professional sports teams. The act of recruiting begins while the prospective candidate is still playing in the collegiate ranks and can even begin as early as high school. Not only is the candidate's performance closely monitored, but also his or her physical health and personal preferences (geographic location, cars, heroes, etc.). Professional teams will then attempt to position themselves in the draft so they will be able to recruit the candidates who they think would contribute most to the team and stand the greatest chance of success in the professional league. They also anticipate what their chances are of successfully recruiting the candidate, including how much the individual will ask to sign with their team and if they are prepared to meet the price. They understand that one of the basic principles of recruiting is that both parties have a choice. For a professional sports team recruitment represents, in many respects, the margin of difference between a successful season and an unsuccessful season: winning a national championship, filling the stands, increasing the value of the franchise, and successfully recruiting other players (building a dynasty).

In many senses, successful recruiting through drafts and trades makes the difference between winners and losers.

At significant turning points of our lives (both personal and professional) we have all been part of the recruitment process. Choice of schools, selection of extracurricular activities, choice of careers, even the choice of spouses—all these turning points in our lives centered around a selection process in which we were either recruiting or being recruited.

Outside the realm of professional sports, there are other "teams" in the world of academia and business which consistently rank at or near the top for achievement in their respective fields. Successful companies recognize that the recruitment process is never ending. Because it is a continuing process, the ultimate goal is to have it run as efficiently as possible. Essential to that efficient functioning is self-knowledge. A company or institution must recognize what it can achieve and admit what it cannot; in addition, it must also know how the individuals it recruits are to serve its present and future needs. This self-awareness is crucial if an organization is to succeed on a long-term basis.

KNOWING YOURSELF

As has been reported, a number of financial institutions are faced with significant portfolio problems as a result of the excesses of the '80s. For some, the resolution of these problems is a matter of life or death. What went wrong? Although greed or outright fraud may have been the basic cause in some instances, in most cases the answer is very simple: not understanding what you are *and* what you are not. In financial circles, companies considering their entry into new markets are encouraged to ask the above question in a slightly different jargon: What is my value added? By this they mean, what is my competitive edge or what will enable me to attract sufficient business on a basis that will yield a profit?

Although this may seem a very basic question, in the frenzied world in which we live it is often overlooked or not viewed objectively. Companies at times observe their peers entering a new market. The herd instinct (rest assured) is just as compulsive on Wall Street as it is in other jungles. Successful recruitment requires the employment of an individual who can apply his skills toward the achievement of an objective a company can realistically attain. Too often companies view the competitive battlefield with rose-tinted glasses. The successes and/or failures of others are not properly evaluated.

Companies at times compound their problems by not only entering a market in which their competitive capabilities are limited, but also by hiring the wrong person. Sound farfetched? Let me give you an example. We are all probably familiar with equipment leasing; in our everyday lives it takes the form of computers, copy machines, and automobiles. However, in the world of high finance there is an aspect of this market known as leveraged leasing. Its focus is the financing of equipment that can cost hundreds of millions of dollars or more. Examples would include commercial aircraft, electric power plants, even satellite transponders in outer space. As you can imagine, the stakes are not only very high, but the transactions are very complex. These transactions also provide a great deal of publicity for both the individuals and companies involved in them as well as profits.

Recently a financial institution decided to enter this arena. However, it became apparent to the individuals the institution interviewed that its abilities (value added) were limited. Unfortunately, the company did not share this perception. It attempted for several months to recruit an outstanding professional to start this new adventure and eventually hired an individual who shared a common characteristic—no knowledge of this financial niche. This sorry marriage, as you might expect, did not last very long. The individual was soon seeking other career options and the company was still trying to determine what went wrong, unwilling to recognize a simple concept, value added.

Unfortunately, this temptation is not limited to the private sector. More than one college and university has heard the "superstar" faculty member siren call. It is easy to fall into the trap. What university would not want a Nobel Laureate or a member of the National Academy of Sciences among its faculty? After all, to have such a prestigious faculty member would help the institution in innumerable ways: aid in recruiting students, serve as a magnet to attract other distinguished faculty members, secure research grants and prestigious national awards, raise alumni pride in their alma mater, help improve fund-raising efforts, increase faculty morale, and have an overall effect of substantially improving the image and reputation of the institution.

Those are good reasons why it makes institutional sense to hire a faculty "superstar." In fact, each reason in and of itself is persuasive; collectively, these reasons are compelling. Now all that has to be done is to go out and successfully recruit such an individual for your school. But where do we start? If this were a normal hire, a good institution, like a good company as mentioned earlier, would identify its strengths (its products) and would pursue an individual who would bring substantially added value to the institution. But in reality it is seldom the case. Unfortunately, most institutions that venture into this arena have not matched their strengths or areas they are interested in building with available "superstars."

Therefore, the question really comes down to whether we are prepared to accept any "superstar," regardless of his or her area of interest, even if the university itself has no strength in that area and may never have thought about building it. Universities who pursue this course quickly discover, like their brethren in the business sector, that they are entering dangerous waters whose temptations and promises may end up providing little more than frustrations and disappointments.

"Superstars" are expensive. Not only is their price high, but so is the price of the support system needed for their care and feeding (teaching assistants, laboratory assistants, equipment, rehabilitation, etc.). When you build a program around one individual, you become extremely vulnerable should that individual decide to leave. Also, just as you were successful in wresting your "superstar" from another institution, you can rest assured that if your individual is any good, he or she will receive an endless series of offers from other schools, some of which will be substantially better than your own. If you don't have in place a critical mass of slightly less-distinguished faculty in your "superstar's" field, research has shown that you stand an excellent chance of losing him or her.

Michael W. Matier (1990) found that among the leading intangible benefits that faculty identified for keeping them at an institution or attracting them to a new one was "reputation of associates." And in the end, if the "superstar" should leave, the institution would be in worse shape than if it had never hired him or her at all. Your skeptics and naysayers will have been vindicated. All the fame and glory instantly vanishes and what is left is a residual feeling of bad will promoted not only by the skeptics and naysayers, but even by some of your supporters who will confess that in their hearts they really did not think it was such a good idea.

While you are right that the path to excellence is through recruiting, it requires careful planning, knowing who you are and who you are not, knowing your strengths and your weaknesses, and being prepared to slowly and methodically take one step at a time.

FINDING THE RIGHT PERSON

Knowing their strengths and weaknesses gives companies and institutions a better understanding of the roles future employees are to fulfill. Relatedly, it gives recruitment efforts specific and appropriate direction. The more focused a company's or institution's recruiting, the better chance each has of finding the people suitable for its needs.

Once a job description has been completed and an individual or group of individuals has been given the responsibility for the recruitment process, the identification of potential candidates begins. To ensure an effective interview and candidate analysis, all recruitment efforts should include the following: (1) a comprehensive résumé from all candidates with a cover letter indicating why they are interested in the position, (2) an initial phone communication with the top five or six candidates probing more deeply into their résumés and reasons for considering the position and location (remember, the phone can be a very efficient and cost-effective organizer for you if used properly), and (3) after the evaluation of the results of phone interviews, reducing the list to the most desirable candidates, and arranging personal interviews for the finalists. Obviously, this process will vary depending on the type and level of position to be filled and whether there are affirmative action, time, or other search procedure requirements to be met.

Yet the above stages of the process do not include all the subtle weighings and balancings done by the recruiter, the institution hiring, and the candidate. It must not be forgotten that successful recruiting requires that both parties say "yes." How the recruiter and the institution he or she represents appears to the candidate is as important as how the candidate appears to the recruiter. In fact, a candidate's belief that the position in question (not to mention the actual company or institution) must be proven worthy of his or her abilities often works to increase the candidate's standing in the eyes of the recruiters. For example, members of a search committee for the presidency of one of the leading research universities underwent an interesting metamorphosis during an encounter with a candidate in the interviewing process. It seems that interviews had been proceeding quite normally with the approach being taken by the members of the search committee that, "We have something valuable (i.e., the presidency of this great university) and you, the candidate, need to convince us why you are good enough for us to choose you for it." That is, all was proceeding along these lines until a certain candidate arrived, and then there was a very interesting role reversal. All of a sudden, the candidate assumed the attitude, "I am good. Convince me why I should come to work at your institution." Simultaneously, the search committee adopted the attitude, "You are the person we want. What do we have to do or say to get you to take the presidency of our school?" (Both found the right answers and eight years later there is still a love affair between the two parties.)

Recruiting is not a one-way street; it is an interactive process in which both employer and prospective employee attempt to discern each other's priorities and values. Not only do the candidate's abilities and the company's or institution's standing come under inspection, but so also do their respective attitudes and opinions. Insofar as the recruiting process generally provides the candidate his or her first acquaintance with a company or institution, recruiting behavior assumes critical importance.

Recent research (Rynes and Miller 1983, Harris and Fink 1987) shows that the recruiter plays a greater role than we might suspect in influencing the candidate's decision. Any recruiter, regardless of whether he or she is engaged in recruiting for the business sector or the higher education sector, conveys in the process of recruiting information about the company and the position being offered. The recruiter also acts as a symbol or example of the quality of individual the company employs, and through his or her actions, reflects the ethos and culture of the company.

In the first role, what we think of as the traditional role of recruiters, the primary responsibility is to convey information to the candidate about the job opportunity in the company and return information to the company about the quality of the candidate, including his or her needs, potential, character, etc. In this capacity the recruiter can influence a candidate's decision by having complete and accurate information about the position and the company or quickly following up with answers to a candidate's questions. Attributes such as being well-informed, accurate, and credible can influence a candidate's choice.

In the second role, the recruiter acts as a company ambassador, reflecting the values and culture of the company. Even a recruiter's personal attributes have been found to influence a candidate's choice. Harris and Fink (1987) found that recruiter characteristics of "personableness, competence, informativeness, and aggressiveness" significantly affected not only the candidate's decision to accept the job, but his or her overall perception of the company.

Like an iceberg, nine-tenths of the recruitment process is beneath the surface. Although an evaluation of a candidate's professional capabilities is an essential step, taking into account the candidate's values and measuring them against the values and culture of the company is critical. Thus, the recruiting process must be expanded to include an evaluation of two additional criteria: (1) the potential match of the candidate with the organization's personality and other individuals, and (2) the individual's outside interests to determine if the community provides appropriate options. The importance of these elements is reflected in the long-term retention rate of companies. We have observed recruitment processes wherein both the candidate and the company spent most of their time discussing the position. This can lead to unexpected problems, especially if an individual and his or her family are very fond of activities for which the environment is unsuitable. If the candidate and his or her family are fond of winter skiing, for example, this should be taken into consideration, especially if the locale is one which does not experience winter. There is a tendency in interviewing for both sides to over-accentuate the positive at times and not probe deeply into potential areas of concern.

Successful recruitment is the culmination of identifying a candidate whose qualifications and interests, both professional and personal, will result in a long-term mutually satisfactory relationship. Much like a marriage, employer and employee go through a honeymoon stage. As this begins to fade, the importance of other subjective elements can reinforce a relationship or accelerate its disintegration.

The importance of the subjective fit of an individual with both the organization and the community must not be underestimated. Some companies take a very paternalistic attitude toward their employees. Having a reputation of this nature can make the recruiting assignment easier. Take the example of a major financial institution in New York City seeking to hire a senior executive with a very specialized background, the proverbial needle in the haystack. A search of this nature would obviously begin by identifying candidates already in New York City or another major metropolitan area—remember the subjective aspects. Unfortunately, this was not successful. To add to the problem, the candidate who possessed these unique qualifications lived with his wife in Arizona. Quite happily, we might add. However, they traveled extensively and had enjoyed the cultural and social aspects of New York City.

Fortunately, a senior executive of the company took a personal role in the recruitment. He met with the candidates and openly discussed any and all questions about the position, the company, and the locale. He informed the candidates that his management style was to regard his employees as part of a family, and his concern for their well-being started with the job but went beyond.

During the recruitment process, he had the opportunity to prove his words were supported by deeds. In the middle of this search, the Arizona candidate's wife became ill and required emergency surgery. The company's senior executive at this time was away on business in Europe. Want to guess who called from Europe to check on her progress and just to say "I care"? Today, some twelve years later, both individuals remain with the same company, one as president and the other as executive vice-president.

It is interesting to note that some of the very best colleges and universities in the country have had similar anecdotal experiences concerning the importance of the personal touch in successfully recruiting the candidate of first choice. For example, it has been reported that at one of our nation's most distinguished citadels of higher education a dean had identified a distinguished educator whom he was trying to recruit to the faculty. The person had made it very clear that he was very happy where he was and was not interested, under any circumstances, in entertaining an offer to change jobs.

A short time later the president of the pursuing university was sitting in the laboratory of the distinguished educator, "pitching" the reluctant candidate. As one could predict, shortly thereafter the distinguished educator was taking up residence in his newfound university.

Do all recruitments end in this fashion? Obviously, that isn't the case. However, the steps indicated herein, if undertaken and performed properly, increase the likelihood of a succesful long-term relationship. Caring and candor can go a long way in this regard.

These two stories, moreover, remind us that the chief executive officer (CEO) is the best recruiter we have in business or on campus. Is this the best use of a CEO's time? We don't know. Perhaps the answer depends upon how much you really want the employee. However, using the CEO as a deal-maker for those difficult cases of recalcitrant candidates conveys the message that the culture of an institution can be characterized by teamwork, perseverance, and determination, attributes which many candidates find very attractive. The culture of the institution is also transmitted by the attitudes and behavior that those below the CEO level take toward the candidate.

Some corporations and universities convey the attitude that there are only two types of employees in the world, those who work for us and those who want to work for us. How else can one explain outrageous and discourteous recruiting behavior such as canceling interviews on short notice, failing to provide feedback to candidates, not communicating with them for months on end, insisting that interviews be scheduled at the recruiter's convenience and not at the candidate's convenience? Instead, they should be trying to limit the number of times the candidate comes to the campus for interviews, inviting the candidate's spouse, and spending as much time selling him or her on the new appointment. More helpful would be letting candidates know the timetable for the recruitment process, being responsive to the request for follow-up information, and allowing the candidate an opportunity to speak to his or her peers who are often, because of their attitude and enthusiasm, a major influence on the candidate's ultimate decision to accept an appointment.

Not only is the recruiter or search committee often perceived as the representative of a company's culture and ethos in general, but they can also be perceived as representing the company's or institution's particular interest (or lack thereof) in a candidate. For example, Rynes and Miller (1983) found that the recruiter's failure to provide certain information about the job "may be interpreted by applicants as, (a) an attempt to evade discussion of unattractive job characteristics, (b) an indication of low recruiter interest in the applicant as a future employee, or (c) both" (p. 153).

Therefore, a prospective candidate may leave the recruitment experience with very negative feelings which might, in fact, be the result of a poorly-prepared recruiter, a poorly-trained recruiter, or a poor recruiter choice. Nonetheless, it may very well be interpreted by a candidate as disinterest on the part of the institution, which is certainly a logical and reasonable conclusion under the circumstances. Therefore, it might make sense for institutions of higher education to learn from the private sector and take the recruitment process a little more seriously than they presently do.

Many institutions currently regard recruiting as something that requires little or no training, and some individuals, for example, deans, automatically chair or serve on search committees by virtue of their office, while others are added to fulfill political (student, alumni) or affirmative action (minority and women) requirements. While we are not arguing against this approach, we are suggesting that it might prove fruitful to spend more time training these individuals on the importance of how to perform their function and the importance of their function. As part of their training they should be alerted to the role they play in communicating information about the institution to the candidate and the effect they can have on the candidate's actual choice to accept the position.

Besides the recruiter, however, there are a number of other factors that can be identified which the candidate considers important in influencing his or her decision to accept an offer. From the business sector we learn that candidates are attracted by money, equipment, visibility, the quality of their colleagues, location, career ladder, taxes (income, property, etc.), cost of living and after-tax income, prestige of the company, and hiring perks.

Increasingly, candidates are influenced by quality-of-life factors. These include close proximity to a major airport, quality of schools, presence of cultural institutions, position for a spouse, size in the community of the candidate's race or ethnic or religious group, the length of the commute to work, the setting of the institution (urban, suburban, rural), cost of housing, the ability of the community to service the special needs of the candidate and/or his or her family.

All these factors go into the equation that the candidate constructs to help determine whether he or she should accept the employment offer. It is also useful to the candidate to determine what it would take for him or her to accept the position. That being the case, it is important to those in institutions of higher education to know which of these factors are important to prospective hires, and if there are others unique to institutions of higher education.

Candidates for positions at institutions of higher education, like their colleagues in the business sector, are attracted by such pecuniary enticements as money (here there are similarities and differences with the business sector), hiring perks (moving expenses, housing assistance, car, memberships), and the nonmonetary issues such as cost of living and taxes, image of the institution, career ladder (prospects for promotion and tenure or administrative advancement), location, equipment, and visibility.

Money includes salary, benefits, travel funds, and an expense account. But for members of institutions of higher education one of the most important benefits, especially for those at private institutions, is free or reduced tuition for members of the candidate's family.

It is also important to note that the relative importance of these tangible benefits of the job differs for individuals in institutions of higher education. Salary may be less important than image of the institution, visibility, career ladder, and equipment.

Similarly, quality-of-life factors are important to candidates for academic positions as well as those in the business world. It should be noted, however, that a position for the spouse, as discussed elsewhere in this book, is more important for prospective academic candidates because of the greater percentage of spouses who have their own careers.

We were also able to identify a number of other factors unique to candidates for positions in higher education that help determine their ultimate decision to accept or reject a position. Studies have shown (Matier 1990a, 1990b; Brakeman 1983; Burke 1988; Smart 1990) those financial benefits which are job-related include potential for making outside income through consulting and other similar activities, summer support, teaching/research load, and research opportunities that in turn might provide secretarial support, graduate assistant support, postdoctoral support, library support, salary override, and so forth.

In addition, there are a number of intangible job-related factors important to job candidates. They include "collegiality, congeniality of associates, reputation of associates, rapport with departmental leaders, reputation of department" (Matier 1990a, p. 10). Those who have studied this field have found that prestige is very importrant to hiring and keeping the best faculty and administrators. Obviously, there is the prestige of the university; but the prestige of the department and of one's colleagues in the department cannot be underestimated. It is this factor that helps explain how departments can rapidly advance in the ranks and just as rapidly decline. Consequently, the following is not an unusual scenario.

A very ambitious, upcoming university successfully recruits a star in a particular field. The star may have a laboratory and a large research grant or grants at the old institution that he or she will either take along to the new institution or attract to it shortly after arriving. In addition, an aggressive institution will take advantage of the magnetic effect of their new star to bring on board other individuals in that field or in the same department. Consequently, a university will very quickly build the department's image and reputation because those in the field soon learn through the academic grapevine of this migration to the institution.

Conversely, many stories can be told of cases when an outstanding individual has been successfully recruited away from an institution and that institution shortly thereafter loses a number of other members from the same department. Consequently, what one should conclude is that the very best in the department or the very best administrators are highly mobile and constantly receive offers from other institutions. There is a very frail balance which keeps them at their institution. A substantial aspect of the equation is the reputation of the associates and the image of the department. Once the balance shifts because a senior member or star leaves, then others become "nervous" and may look with renewed interest at offers they have received and are receiving.

It's good to keep in mind that an institution that is preeminent in its field is the hardest to recruit from—and the easiest to recruit for. Top-notch individuals who believe they are working for a "champion" are convinced that any other opportunity would be a step down. While remuneration may be a factor in luring them away, it is the regard in which the institution is held that determines whether they stay. Developing and maintaining a feeling that we are all part of the best team provides a tremendous advantage in both retaining current employees and attracting prospective candidates.

CONCLUSION

Let us conclude as we began by returning to our analogy of the recruiting strategies employed by professional sports teams. There are a number of lessons colleges and universities can learn from professional sports teams as they develop and improve their own recruiting strategies. Let's look at a few.

First, colleges and universities should know the recruiting cycle and use it to their advantage. There are natural times of the year when the best candidates become available or at least become psychologically vulnerable to an offer to move. Here we are talking about more than the traditional, newly-minted Ph.D. or postdoctorate who starts to look for his or her first assistant professorship. For senior officers, graduation represents the closure of the academic year. At that point, they have not begun to gear up for the new year, which takes place in August. Therefore, one of the best times to approach a prospective dean or other full or associate professor, Nobel Prize winner, or National Academy member may very well be in June.

Second, keep track of candidates in whom you are interested and seize upon opportunities. Professional sports teams do this by tracking individuals from high school to college and up through the minor leagues. Then when they are prepared to draft or trade they know not only who they want, but who they have the best chance of signing. Similarly, institutions of higher education should keep track of outstanding faculty and administrators who, given the right circumstance, they would like to attract to their institution. In addition, colleges and universities should keep track of institutions that are having financial difficulty and individuals who are unhappy in their current situation. (Perhaps there is a new dean, provost, or president with whom our targeted individual is having difficulty getting along.) Personal situations also change (i.e., divorce), which might encourage the individual to consider leaving.

Many argue that faculty accept new positions primarily because they want to leave their old job rather than because of the attraction of the new job (Caplow and McGee 1958; Toombs and Malier 1981; Gartshore, Hibbard, and Stockard 1983; Matier 1990).

Third, remember that it is cheaper to hire future stars than superstars. Keep track of potential National Academy members and recruit them while they are on the way up.

Fourth, develop a recruiting plan—goals, objectives, assigned responsibilities, deadlines. It is most important to have good communication with all parties on the team, making sure that they fully buy into the strategy and what the institution stands for. For example, the hiring of stars is something that requires not only a commitment by the president, provost, dean, and department chair, but also by the faculty in the department. We have seen numerous occasions where the president has declared his or her intention to go out and hire star faculty, committed large sums of endowment money, and spent the next two years in frustration wondering why it did not happen. It did not happen because not everyone on the team believed that this was an appropriate course for the institution to follow and, therefore, made halfhearted attempts at best to comply with the president's directive.

Please do not be put off by what may sound more crass or commercial than what we are used to hearing in institutions of higher education. The reality is that success requires the ability and willingness to seize upon opportunities that present themselves.

Fifth, before you start recruiting, know what you want, how much it is going to cost to get it, and be prepared to pay the price. Many institutions are naive in assuming how much it would cost to recruit an outstanding faculty member, dean, provost, vice-president, or president. As the saying goes, "If you want to be in the big leagues, you have to be prepared to pay to play." Or as a Ferrari dealer once told a prospective customer, "If you have to ask the price, you can't afford to buy it."

Sixth, it is important that institutions remember that the goal is to build a winning team. One superstar does not make a department. Even if you are successful in recruiting the individual, in some sense that is the easy part because you also have to be prepared to keep the individual. The rule of thumb is that in order to have a superstar faculty member, an institution should have a critical mass in that individual's area that includes full professors, associate professors, assistant professors, postdoctorates, etc. Among the primary reasons identified by faculty for being attracted to new institutions or for refusing offers to leave old institutions is the reputation of the department and the quality of their colleagues.

Finally, we need to think about where to recruit. To pursue the simile, what are higher education's farm clubs? Certainly the private sector comes immediately to mind. Corporate research laboratories that win their share of prestigious scientific awards represent an excellent source for faculty. The federal government, including the military, represents an excellent source of clinical/medical faculty members. Foreign countries similarly represent a good place to recruit; we find many times that the faculty members have been trained at some of the most prestigious American universities.

While the above steps will help to improve an institution's recruiting process, it must be remembered that for all the information and advice offered here and elsewhere about recruiting, it still remains a complex process. Because it is ultimately a transaction between individuals, each recruitment process is unique; its failures and successes always differ in particulars, if not in kind. That there is no one successful method which would apply to all situations is perhaps the most frustrating aspect of recruitment. What we have tried to offer are guidelines drawn from the experiences of those familiar with the complexities of recruiting. However, it must be emphasized that they can function only as guidelines. As to what the best recruiting process is for a particular company or institution of higher learning, only the company or institution itself can make that decision.

REFERENCES

Brakeman, L. F. 1983. "Hiring and Keeping the Best Faculty." In J. W. Fuller (ed.), *Issues in Faculty Personnel Policies* (pp. 5–19). *New Directions for Higher Education,* No. 41. San Francisco: Jossey-Bass.

Burke, D. L. 1988. *A New Academic Marketplace.* New York: Greenwood Press.

Caplow, T., and R. J. McGee. 1958. *The Academic Marketplace.* New York: Basic Books.

Gartshore, R. J., M. Hibbard, and J. Stockard. 1983. *Factors Affecting*

Mobility at the University of Oregon. Eugene, Oreg.: University of Oregon Press.

Harris, M. M., and S. L. Fink. 1987. "A Field Study of Applicant Reactions to Employment Opportunities: Does the Recruiter Make a Difference?" *Personnel Psychology* 40: 865–84.

Matier, M. W. 1990a. "Recruiting Faculty: Complementary Tales from Two Campuses" [Paper presented at the Annual Forum of the Association for Institutional Research, Louisville, Ky]. (ERIC Document Reproduction Service No. ED 308 786).

————. 1990b. "Retaining Faculty: A Tale of Two Campuses." *Research in Higher Education* 31 (1): 39–60.

Rynes, S. L., and H. E. Miller. 1983. "Recruiter and Job Influences on Candidates for Employment." *Journal for Applied Psychology* 68: 147–54.

Smart, J. C. 1990. "A Causal Model of Faculty Turnover Intentions." *Research in Higher Education* 31 (5): 405–422.

Toombs, W., and J. Marlier. 1981. "Career Change Among Academics: Dimensions of Decision" [Paper presented at the Annual Meeting of the American Educational Research Association, Los Angeles, Calif.] (ERIC Document Reproduction Service No. ED 202 423).

10

The Pros and Cons
of Using Headhunters

Judith Block McLaughlin

In the classified section in the middle pages of the *Chronicle of Higher Education* each week, a new last line has begun to appear in some job listings. "Nominations and applications should be sent to Such-and-such consulting firm," these notices state. This single phrase reveals a sign of changing times in the hiring process in higher education. Although only a small portion of advertisements mention a consultant, many other institutions also conduct their searches with professional assistance. Indeed, the increase in the use of consultants in searches is probably the most remarkable development in recent years in the search process for college and university administrators.

"What *is* a search consultant?" was the question frequently posed to me ten years ago when I mentioned that I was intrigued by the emerging use of professional consultants in searches for college presidents. Search consultants, if known at all, were thought of as

Acknowledgment is due to the Christian A. Johnson Endeavor Foundation for their funding of this research on the use of consultants in searches.

corporate headhunters who occasionally raided college and university faculties or administration for better paying jobs outside of higher education. Today, by contrast, approximately 60 percent of college and university presidential searches are assisted by professional search consultants, and this use of consultants is filtering down to all levels of the academy. Instead of wondering what a consultant is, many people now have their own stories, good and bad, about the search consultants they have known or known of.

A fixture in corporate and industrial hiring for decades, executive recruiters made their initial forays into the hiring process in higher education with presidential searches and with those second-tier administrative positions most resembling positions in the for-profit sector, jobs such as treasurer, vice-president for financial affairs, vice-president of development, and director of computer services. The keen competition for skilled people for these positions—competition not only within higher education but also with the for-profit sector with its lure of higher remuneration—motivated employers to seek help in searching for prospects. Often, too, the people conducting the hiring process for these positions were among those most familiar with the use of consultants for specialized tasks and therefore the least resistant to the idea of employing a consultant in the higher education hiring process. For much the same reasons, the first places on the academic side of the campus to use search consultants were those positions hardest to fill because of competition from outside the academy, searches for deans of medical schools and deans of business schools. They were followed in rapid succession by searches for provosts and academic vice-presidents, searches for deans of other professional schools, and, most recently, searches for other vice-presidencies and for academic and administrative deanships.

The reasons for this rapid change in hiring practice are many. Searches are now almost always national in scope, and this wide advertising typically results in extensive paperwork that needs attention. Search consultants are sometimes brought on board to help to manage the process more efficiently and expeditiously. The increased use of consultants also stems from the experience of many search committees that it is difficult to find good people for the job. Not infrequently, the decision to bring a search consultant on board may be made after the search is well under way, when the committee looks over the responses to their advertising of the vacancy and is unhappy with the quality of applicants for the position. Sometimes, a search consultant is seen as helping an institution achieve greater breadth in its candidate pool. Search committee members may hope that the consultant will enable them to find prospects outside of their usual hunting grounds, perhaps in institutions not in their immediate circles or even outside of higher education altogether. Increasingly, search committees wish to identify promising women and minority candidates. Recognizing this, many search consultants now advertise this as a special service that they can provide a search committee.

Search consultants may also be more attractive these days because of the recognition that hiring mistakes can be exceedingly costly, especially in pivotal positions in the institution. Hence the fee of the consultant, sometimes balked at by institutions eager to keep the cost of searches as low as possible, may seem small in comparison to the expense of launching another search or suffering through the trauma of a poor selection.

The increased use of consultants is also due no doubt to the recent proliferation in consultants available to advise higher education searches. At the presidential level, no sooner has a president announced his or her intended departure than an array of search firms make known their interest in assisting with the search for a successor. As one search committee chair commented, "Not only did we receive a slew of letters from candidates in response to our advertisement, we also received a large number of letters and brochures from search consultants who wanted us to employ them to do the search." Even those search committee members who gave no thought to a search consultant now have the possibility presented persuasively to them. Thus, there is a complicated interaction at work here: the emerging use of search consultants in higher education motivates new players to enter the consulting field (both corporate consultants who now see higher education as a virtually untapped market, and former college presidents and senior administrators who view this new area of employment as a natural next step in their career trajectory). And the expansion of consultants who see higher education as their catchment area raises the profile of search consultants generally and makes them more likely to be considered in the hiring process.

CONSULTANTS: THE CONTRIBUTIONS

The fact that search consultants have proliferated is in itself no argument for using one! What can be gained by employing a search consultant? What sort of assistance might they offer a hiring officer or search committee? According to a great many search committee chairs and members, search consultants can be extraordinarily helpful in many aspects of the search and selection process. Experts in the art of recruiting, search consultants can advise search committee members who are often amateurs and who are always busy with the simultaneous pressures of their job and the search.

Navigating the Process

Depending on when consultants enter the search process, they may find a search already under way or one not yet fully delineated. Most consultants prefer the latter scenario, since this allows them to advise a committee or hiring authority at the outset about how to structure the search and what sort of individual to consider for the position. Many search committees are unrealistic about the length of time it will take to identify promising candidates and to evaluate their viability for the position. Committee members may not appreciate the extent of work required in responding to inquiries and processing papers. Experienced recruiters, search consultants can navigate the search process for busy committee members, suggesting where to place advertisements and whom to call upon for nominations, pointing out along the way important details that might otherwise be overlooked, planning the logistical arrangements and managing their implementation.

Consultants can be especially helpful in educating search committee members about the importance of confidentiality during the search process and alerting them as to what measures should be taken to avoid unwanted disclosure. The leaks that damage searches, and, sometimes, candidates' careers, often happen unwittingly, because search committee members are inexperienced at dealing with the press or because of oversights in the mechanics of the search. One presidential search committee, for example, intended to keep the names of candidates confidential. However, all mailings were sent to candidates' offices, rather than to their homes. Moreover, the search committee's printed stationery had the return address, "XYZ University Presidential Search Committee," and the word "CONFI-DENTIAL" was stamped in large letters across the front of the envelope!

Drafting the Position Description

Typically, advertisements of a position vacancy include a capsule description of the qualifications being sought in candidates for the position. Although some readers pay little attention to these statements and apply even though they possess few if any of the items cited, the criteria do serve to screen out prospects. Yet many position descriptions contain qualifications that are not really essential for success in the job, or are so vague or generic that they tell little about what sort of person is desired. Having seen many such descriptions before, the consultant can help the search committee define the criteria in a way that alerts readers to the qualifications required and helps the members of the search committee arrive at a better understanding of the nature of the job and the characteristics needed in the jobholder.

A consultant will usually develop the position description only after extensive interviewing with members of the search committee and other key institutional personnel. Many consultants believe that this "pre-search study" or "institutional needs analysis" is one of the most significant contributions they can provide an institution. As the Academic Search Consultation Service (1991) explains, "Our initial study for the search committee is also invaluable to the person eventually appointed, since anyone stepping into a new leadership position needs to learn quickly the answers to the same questions. What are the needs of this institution? What are most important? What are the expectations of the governing board, faculty, staff, students, alumni, and community leaders?"

Strengthening the Pool

For many search committees, the chief reason to employ professional assistance is to enhance the candidate pool. The search consultant is expected to locate candidates who would not likely be identified in the normal channels utilized by the search committee. Hence, consultants are seen as "headhunters," whose primary purpose is to bring in a bounty of high-caliber candidates. As mentioned earlier, in recent years the concern about affirmative action has meant that search consultants are turned to increasingly to find "nontraditional" candidates for positions, especially women and minorities. Sometimes the consultant's success is measured in actual numbers: "The search consultant added more than twenty names to our candidate pool." Consultants are assumed—oftentimes incorrectly—to have a "stable" of candidates they can draw upon, or, more accurately, to have extensive professional networks they can pluck to produce the names of prospects.

Evaluating Candidates

Once a pool of candidates has been developed, a search committee or hiring officer must investigate, evaluate, and court these candidates. Here, a consultant can play an important role as intermediary, assessing the paper credentials and gathering additional background information from a variety of sources, talking with candidates directly, and learning more about them indirectly. Depending on the wishes of the search committee, the consultant may be the primary contact with candidates, or may remain in the background, leaving the committee chair or hiring officer to speak with candidates about their involvement in the search. In either case, the consultant typically sees it as his or her responsibility to ensure that candidates are treated courteously during the search, informed of their status in the process, made aware of the approximate timetable to be followed, and educated about the nature of the job and the institutional context in which it is situated. Search consultants will generally advise a search committee on what kinds of questions they should ask in their interviews and what potential weak areas of candidates they ought to explore. Some consultants will sit in on search committee interviews, occasionally asking questions or simply being present as silent observers. Other consultants believe strongly that their presence in the room is inappropriate, that it detracts from the bonding of candidate and committee, or that it prevents them from approaching candidates and committee members afterward to inquire as to how the interview proceeded. One consultant explained that he gets his best data on candidates by comparing their sense of the meeting with that of the members of the search committee, and if he were in the room during the interview, the candidate would not be as forthcoming, remarking that "you were there, so you know." Other consultants argue that their presence during the interview is an important check on the process, in terms of their ability to discuss their impressions of candidates with search committee members and to intervene during the interview itself if it is being poorly managed.

Among the candidates in the pool, frequently, are one or more internal candidates: faculty members or administrators (or, occasionally, trustees) at the college or university. Assessing the strength of internal candidates for a position can be a particularly sticky business. Here, a consultant can be of great use, gathering information about how the internal candidate or candidates are viewed within and outside of the institution and evaluating them in comparison to others in the competition. The consultant may also help to legitimate the search if an internal candidate is chosen, disabusing skeptics of the notion that "it was wired from the start." As one faculty member commented, "I guess it was a *real* search after all, or otherwise they wouldn't have spent all that money on a consultant."

Conducting Background Investigations

Occasionally, a consultant will be brought on board in the final days of the search to conduct a thorough background check on a small group of finalists or a final candidate. The consultant is recognized as experienced in making reference inquiries, knowing whom to call and what to ask, how to probe beyond the usual platitudes, and what to make of contradictory assessments. A few of the larger executive recruiting firms have hired private detectives to ferret out information on candidates so that the hiring institution is not embarrassed by some scandal or dark secret a candidate has not divulged.

Serving as Go-Between

Just as consultants may serve as an intermediary between candidates and the hiring institution throughout the course of the search process, so they can play an important role as go-between as the process nears conclusion. As the number of candidates is winnowed, the questions of those remaining in the pool increase. Many of these have to do with the terms of the appointment. In addition to the obvious questions regarding salary and starting date, many other details—from benefits to housing, from staff to spousal consider-ations—may determine the success of the search effort. If the nego-tiations do not proceed smoothly, the top choice or choices of the search committee may turn down the position. In this era of two-professional couples, for example, the professional options available for the candidate's spouse may be the wild card on which the effort to recruit a particular candidate depends. Having a third party assist with conversations about such matters can allow both sides to be candid without worrying about causing offense, and may allow for compromises or creative alternatives that neither party to the nego-tiations would be sufficiently objective enough to come up with on his or her own. In one presidential search, the search chair was a lawyer whose specialty is labor law and who often serves as an arbitrator. Believing himself an expert in negotiations, he scoffed at the idea of using a consultant in the final discussions with the can-didate who was the search committee's top choice for the presidency. But the search chair failed to realize that as one of the parties to the negotiation he became invested in his own position and lost the freedom to range back and forth between the two differing perspec-tives. As a result, the negotiations broke down over a matter which, many months later, the candidate himself thought of a way it might have been satisfactorily resolved, and the institution found itself in the position of having to start the search process all over again.

CONSULTANTS: THE CRITICISM

Although a great many search committees and hiring officers have high praise for the search consultant they employed, not all have had such positive experiences. Occasionally, a search committee will report that the consultant they used provided them little service and presented them large bills. In some instances, the criticism is even stronger, with the hiring institution or the candidates in the search expressing distinct displeasure with the consultation experience.

By and large, the problems identified with consultants fall into three categories. The first group includes complaints with the work of the consultant, a second set of issues has to do with the interaction of consultant and search committee, and the third are dilemmas intrinsic to the nature of the consultation profession.

Unsatisfactory Performance

The search consultation industry is intensely competitive. Consultants make their living by bringing in clients, and their remuneration typically is linked to the salary of the person being recruited (generally one-third of the first-year cash compensation). The greater the financial overhead of the firm, the greater the income that must be generated to cover expenses.

Search consulting, if done well, is extremely time-consuming work. It requires many hours of learning about the institution, getting to know the hiring officer or members of the search committee, developing a mutual understanding of the important qualifications needed for the job, contacting possible nominators and nominees, interviewing and investigating candidates, and working with the hiring institution to bring closure to the search process. Search consulting in higher education is especially time-consuming, because the concept of shared governance requires touching base with all important constituencies. But some consultants simply don't spend the time they should with each individual search. Perhaps they are trying to juggle too many searches at once; perhaps another search has captured their attention because it is inherently more interesting, financially more lucrative, or encountering unanticipated problems; perhaps, as a newcomer to higher education searches, they do not fully appreciate the culture and mores of academe. The result is that the search gets shortchanged; the consultant does not follow through on leads, fails to keep in touch with candidates, or proceeds with an insufficient understanding of the institution or the nature of the position being filled. The latter is particularly hazardous, because a consultant who does not have a good appreciation of the culture of the college or university and the nuances of the job may misrepresent the position to candidates or misjudge their appropriateness or lack of fit.

Although the most common complaint about poor performance relates to the lack of time spent on the search, other criticisms concern the person who is doing the consulting. Like all professionals, search consultants are not all equally good at their work. Some consultants are better organizers of the process than they are evaluators of people; some are better "anthropologists" than others, more able to figure out the culture and the mores of each particular institution. Moreover, each consultant has his or her own personality and working style which may, or may not, mesh well with the search committee or hiring officer. Just as the "chemistry" between candidate and institution must be right for the new appointment to work out successfully, so the consultant and search committee must also be compatible if the consultation relationship is going to be beneficial.

Interaction of Consultant with Committee

As the involvement of consultants in searches has proliferated, the criticism of this practice has increased as well. One particular concern expressed relates to the change that a consultant can cause in the dynamic of the search process. Robert Birnbaum believes that a consultant "short-circuits the learning process" when the consultant screens the candidates instead of the search committee (Leatherman 1991). Although this form of assistance may expedite the search process, the danger in having the consultant play such a major role in evaluating candidates is that members of the search committee may gain only a filtered sense of how others view their institution and what range of candidates are included among the available possibilities. Throughout the search process, the entry of the consultant into search committee discussions may disrupt the conversations between members. Some committee members may feel less free to voice their opinions in the presence of an outsider and a recognized expert on searches. Additionally, the conversation may become directed mostly to the consultant, rather than an exchange between members. Finally, if the consultant is the chief spokesman in deliberations with candidates, the candidates may develop bonds with the consultant rather than with the members of the search committee. Although further research is still needed in this area, it behooves both the consultant and the search committee chair to monitor closely committee discourse and activities in order to make certain that the consultant is not preempting but merely, in Nancy Archer-Martin's words, "support[s], not supplant[s] the work of the search committee" (1990).

Professional and Ethical Issues

Search consultants have their own professional associations and their own rules regarding ethical practice. Among the latter is a "keep away" policy regarding any individual the consultant has placed or any organization the consultant has advised. As *Fortune* magazine explained, "it is an ironclad rule among the Big Six that when a corporation hires them to find an executive, for at least two years thereafter no executive working for the client corporation will be recruited for a job at any other client corporation" (Meyer 1978). A second principle of operating in many firms is that the firm will not proceed in more than one search with the same candidate.

Both of these policies have direct implications for the candidate pool available to a search committee using a consultant. Presumably, a consultant cannot recommend a dean who is at a college the consultant has recently advised for a job at another institution the consultant is now assisting. Since candidates come into the search process from a number of directions, however, this policy seems not to interfere with recruitment. Although the dean may not be on the consultant's list, she may be nominated by someone else or apply directly. When James McComas, who was president of the University of Toledo for three years, was named president of Virginia Tech, Heidrick & Struggles consultant John Richmond explained in the consultant industry newsletter, *Executive Recruiter News,* that he had not recommended McComas for either search, and his job as consultant at Toledo and Virginia Tech had been to enrich the pool of candidates, not to recommend a final choice (1988).

The operation of the second principle, that of not continuing with the same candidate in more than one search a firm is assisting, is potentially more problematic. In the large firms which utilize computer networks, a consultant is informed by computer that a file the consultant is retrieving is being used simultaneously by another consultant in the firm. The two consultants then discuss the situation, determine which institution seems a better fit for the candidate, and then proceed with the candidate's name only in that one search. By avoiding internal competition within the firm, the firm confronts a case of conflict of interest with institutions and candidates. Had one or both institutions not been using consultants or using consultants from different firms, they might well have kept the candidate on both lists, conceivably both proceeding to make an offer to this candidate, and leaving the choice up to the candidate. Some institutions have gotten wise to the risk of this conflict of interest and now inquire of firms prior to hiring them as to what comparable institutions and similar positions the firm is serving as consultant. Just this past year, for example, Swarthmore chose not to use Korn/Ferry International, Inc. because Brandeis and Grinnell had already employed the firm for their presidential searches.

The policy of not proceeding with one candidate in two searches is not necessarily followed by not-for-profit firms. As Charles B. Neff of the Presidential Search Consultation Service explains, "We do not have any trouble in involving a candidate in more than one search at a time. We are frank with both institutions and with the candidates about what is going on. Our position is that both institutions are looking for the right fit between the candidate and the institution. Whereas it is possible that the candidate will fit both institutions, it is more likely that the candidate will fit one better than the other. If the proper choice is made, both institutions are better off" (personal communication May 9, 1991).

Another ethical question concerns the influence that a consultant may have over the outcome of the search. It is, of course, the institution that makes the hiring decision, and good consultants are careful to pull back from making recommendations about who should be selected. Nevertheless, the consultant's assessment of candidates throughout the search process can affect who is chosen. In some searches, the consultant will be asked to screen large stacks of candidate papers and recommend a smaller group for the institution to consider. Some consultants make the first contacts with candidates, providing the hiring institution a précis on each serious prospect. Frequently the consultant is asked to conduct reference checks and to give the search committee a synopsis of what has been learned. As noted earlier, the consultant can provide a very great service in all of these areas. But the potential power of the consultant vis-à-vis the evaluation of candidates can occasionally be worrisome. For consultants, like all of us, have their own biases. A search consultant who has a particular favorite candidate could sway a search committee in his or her direction, and, conversely, a search consultant who dislikes a candidate could discourage the committee from giving this person a closer look. The danger is that a consultant who assists in a large number of searches could conceivably block this candidate's chances in all these searches. Several people believe that this has happened to them, having learned from repeated episodes that they do not advance very far in searches where a particular consultant is involved, as opposed to others where the consultant is not assisting the process. Of course, a consultant's having prior information about a candidate or candidates may be beneficial to a search committee. A consultant who assisted a search for a president of a small Catholic college came across an application whose cover letter began: "Dear Sir: I am a devout Catholic." Several months later, the same consultant was employed by the search committee of a Calvinist college. Imagine his surprise when he came across a letter from the "devout Catholic" which, this time, began: "Dear Sir: I am a devout Calvinist."

MAKING THE CHOICE

The best way to minimize the risks of using a consultant and obtain the maximum advantages is to choose the consultant carefully. There is presently a large roster of choices, including single consultants who operate independently, small "boutiques," larger firms with a national focus, and large, international corporate firms. There are firms with specializations in higher education, or even in one particular kind of higher education search (e.g., presidential searches, or searches for development or admissions officers), as well as firms that consult with business and industry and have only recently taken on an academic clientele. The names of many consultants and consulting firms are easily obtained by contacting colleges and universities that have recently conducted searches for comparable positions. This is also an excellent means of gathering information about the performance of the consultant during the search. Did he or she follow through as the search chair had expected? What sort of services did the consultant provide? Were there any misunderstandings or disagreements, and if so, what about?

Once a search committee or hiring officer has identified a number of possible consultants, the next step is to procure information directly from them. In addition to getting the consultant or firm's brochure, many colleges and universities are engaging in "shoot-outs" to compare competing firms and individuals. A "shoot-out," in the consultant industry lingo, is an occasion at which several consultants are invited to make competitive presentations of the services they would render the hiring institution. For many search committees, the "shoot-out" not only helps committee members determine which search consultant they wish to employ; it also serves as a practice run for the committee in interviewing and evaluating people.

The decision as to consultant is preceded by an assessment of what a hiring officer or search committee desires in the way of assistance. Some consultants have particular ways of managing a search and are not amenable to changing these procedures. Others are willing to provide only a partial service, if this is all a committee wants, or to amend their usual modus operandi to fit a hiring institution's preferred scheme. The expectations of hiring institution and consultant should be discussed at length before the consultation agreement is reached. What will the consultant do? How often will the consultant meet with the search committee, and how available will he or she be outside of these sessions?

Clarification is also needed as to who in a consulting firm will be handling the search. In some larger firms, a senior partner is sent as the marketing representative to the "shoot-out," but another member of the firm will actually be assigned the work of recruiting. Since, in the end, the success of the consultation experience depends on the caliber of individual doing the consulting, it is important to choose the individual consultant as well as the firm.

As many institutions know well, the use of a search consultant provides no guarantee of a successful outcome to a search. In the best of cases, however, the consultant provides expertise and assistance that enables the search committee or hiring officer to organize and implement a thorough search process and to make a thoughtful and informed selection.

REFERENCES

Academic Search Consultation Service. 1991. Brochure. Washington, D.C.: ASCS.

Archer-Martin, Nancy. 1990. *Building the Leadership Team: Thoughts on Administrative Search*. Nantucket, Mass.: Educational Management Network.

Dennis, Lawrence J. 1988. "Colleges Should Be Wary of Using Headhunters to Fill Their Top Jobs." *The Chronicle of Higher Education* (January 27).

Executive Recruiter News (September 1988): 7.

Fisher, Charles F. 1978. *Developing and Evaluating Administrative Leadership*. San Francisco: Jossey-Bass Inc.

Fisher, James L. 1991. *The Board and the President*. New York: American Council on Education and Macmillan.

Garrison, Stephen A. 1989. *Institutional Search: A Practical Guide to Executive Recruiting in Nonprofit Organizations*. New York: Praeger.

Gee, E. Gordon. 1991. "The Dual-Career Couple." *Educational Record* (Winter): 45–47.

Goldsmith, James. 1990. *"Executive Recruiters in Presidential Searches."* Doctoral Dissertation, University of Nevada, Las Vegas.

Heller, Scott. 1987. "A Headhunter Helps Dartmouth—and Many Others—To Find a New President." *The Chronicle of Higher Education* 33, no. 32 (April 22): 1, 14–17.

Leatherman, Courtney. 1991. "Presidential Searches Said to Offer Colleges Chance to Take Stock." *The Chronicle of Higher Education* 37, no. 25 (March 6): A–11.

Marchese, Theodore J. 1988. *The Search Committee Handbook: A Guide to Recruiting Administrators*. Washington, D.C.: American Association for Higher Education.

———. 1989. "Search from the Candidate's Perspective: An Interview with Maria M. Perez." *American Association for Higher Education Bulletin* 42, no. 4 (December): 3–5, 11–13.

McLaughlin, Judith Block. 1985. "Plugging the Leaks: Maintaining Confidentiality in the Search for a President." *Association of Governing Boards of Universities and Colleges Reports* 27, no. 3 (May/June): 24–30.

———. 1992. "Selecting the Chief Executive." In Richard T. Ingram and Associates, *Handbook of Public College and University Trusteeship* and *Handbook of Private College and University Trusteeship*. San Francisco: Jossey-Bass Inc.

McLaughlin, Judith Block, and David Riesman. 1990. *Choosing a College President: Opportunities and Constraints*. Washington, D.C.: The Carnegie Foundation for the Advancement of Teaching.

Meyer, Herbert E. 1978. "The Headhunters Come Upon Golden Days." *Fortune* (October 9).

Mottram, Richard A. 1983. "Executive Search Firms as an Alternative to Search Committees." *Educational Record* 64 (Winter): 38–42.

Nason, John, with Nancy Axelrod. 1984. *Presidential Search: A Guide to the Process of Selecting College and University Presidents.* Washington, D.C.: Association of Governing Boards of Universities and Colleges.

Rent, George. 1987. "A Case for the Search Consultant." *Administration: The Management Newsletter for Higher Education* 6, no. 18 (September 28): 1.

Riesman, David, and Judith Block McLaughlin. 1984. "A Primer on the Use of Consultants in Presidential Recruitment." *Change* (September): 12–23.

Sibbald, John. 1990. *The Career Makers: America's Top 100 Executive Recruiters.* New York: Harper Business.

Touchton, Judith G. 1989. " 'Maybe We Need a Search Firm?' Questions to Ask Yourself and Your Consultant." *American Association for Higher Education Bulletin* 42, no. 4 (December): 6–9.

Wergin, Jon F. 1989. *Consulting in Higher Education: Principles for Institutions and Consultants.* Washington, D.C.: Association of American Colleges.

11

Conclusion

Stephen Joel Trachtenberg

THE DARKENING CONTEXT

Every book has its own history—from initial idea to formal publication—and this one is no exception to the rule. It was conceived at a time when there were some obvious storm clouds gathering over our schools of higher education. Serious financial problems alone, such as were beginning to confront most universities and four-year colleges, made it clear that hiring practices in the academic world, hitherto often conducted in a spirit of debonair informality not unlike that which is said to have once prevailed around the roulette wheels of Monte Carlo, were going to have to be "shaped up"—and fast.

As the individual chapters began to come in from our various colleagues, the storm clouds steadily and remorselessly thickened. "In these difficult economic times," Joseph Kauffman noted in his discussion of the president's role in the hiring process, "there will definitely be some reductions and reallocation of funds and positions." And by the time his and the other contributions were being set in type, the heavens had unleashed winds of hurricane force on presidents, vice-presidents, deans, and faculty members alike, and the rain of bad news would have daunted even a modern Noah and perhaps even a contemporary Job.

The pace was set, in many ways, by the public sector of higher education. As state after state found it increasingly difficult to keep up with its citizens' needs for health care, adequate elementary and secondary education, and police protection, cutbacks aimed at state universities and colleges seemed to come in volleys rather than mere individual broadsides. That "adjustments" in state higher education budgets might now be levied two or even three times a year surprised no one. Governors, as they imposed "caps" on academic spending, used the kind of tough talk formerly reserved for dealing with drug dealers or other malefactors. And in the most hard-pressed states—like Connecticut, where I spent eleven years as a university president in the 1970s and 1980s—discussion increasingly focused on the "financial exigency" clauses in faculty contracts that would make it possible to fire even teachers with tenure.

As 1991 drew toward a close, the print and electronic media confirmed, from a national perspective, what Americans had seen developing on a state-by-state basis. Tuition at the "publics" had risen by well over 12 percent in the past year. At the "independents," meanwhile, tuitions were up by close to 7 percent. Though a very considerable gap remained, state universities and colleges had lost a certain edge and were seeing some even grimmer handwriting on the wall. Letters to the editor in regional and local newspapers were beginning to question the very idea of "income-blind" tuition rates at public institutions—the famous "bargains" enjoyed by middle- and upper-income families, which only a few senior administrators from the independent sector have challenged even as recently as the 1980s. And as Lewis C. Solmon and Cheryl L. Fagnano document in chapter six of this book, salary increases at public institutions, as the 1990s dawned, were already trailing those of their private competitors, with inevitable representations about faculty quality and morale "never being lower"—effects compounded in more recent years by the sense that where state-controlled budgets are concerned, "anything is now possible."

Worse yet, front-page stories about steeply rising tuition at the "publics" vied for space with the news about cutbacks, the thinning-out of support staff, larger class sizes, and postponements in badly needed renovations. The condition of the *national* economy, meanwhile, was also hitting these schools, especially in areas like New England and the Northeast. Jobs were harder to find, harder to keep; tuition fees, therefore, more of a challenge for families struggling with "basic expenses." Hard-pressed companies were no longer as actively in the market for continuing education. Admissions staff, never in generous supply at public institutions—"Why bother?" might once have summarized the prevailing attitude—were having to be reduced at a time when they were finally needed.

But those on the payrolls of private universities and colleges had little reason to kick up their heels or break out the champagne. The American economy was hitting them in identical or closely related ways. Declines in federal and state funding increasingly affected *their* budgets, too. And the saddest fact of all about American higher education was one they fully shared with their public siblings: the fact that a steady diet of academic "scandals," ranging from padded research overhead to "political correctness" and what some writers termed the general "dumbing" of America, had reduced public confidence and trust in this country's universities and colleges to their lowest levels of the twentieth century. That boded especially ill for the *future* of higher education budgets, private *or* public.

What had been highly advisable when *The Art of Hiring* was first conceived—that hiring practices be made rational enough to withstand inspection—had become, as the year 1991 gave way to 1992, a matter of grim necessity. Either the best people would be hired in the best possible way or a school might well find itself getting yet another push on the downward slope. Universities and colleges would either learn to deal with what M. Fredric Volkmann calls, in this book, "the increasingly contentious and sometimes litigious atmosphere in which the interviewing and screening process must operate" or, in a variety of unpleasant ways, they would find themselves *being dealt with.*

Given the speed with which events develop in our incredibly fast-paced world, there's no telling how bad things will have become, or whether some "miraculous" respite may have taken place, at the time when you, the individual reader, hold this book in your hands. What is certain is that our contributors have "done themselves proud" and have put together a truly synoptic volume on a very difficult subject, at a very difficult moment in the history of American higher education. Even the most optimistic forecasts make it unlikely that the subject with which this volume is concerned will have slipped into irrelevance soon, if ever again.

THROUGH MY EYES

As the climate in which American universities and colleges must function has turned icy, turbulent, and dangerous, and as fiscal cutbacks have reduced the ranks of academic administrators and staff members, the hiring process—together with admissions, development, and budgetary planning—has taken on an urgency that would have seemed inconceivable five or ten years ago. Payrolls that once rose unabashedly skyward now look tight and limited. Rightly or wrongly, each "hire" seems to threaten a "fire." Hiring procedures, once so casual and informal, must now be conducted in a spirit of caution—able to withstand scrutiny from whatever direction scrutiny may come.

"Ay, there's the rub!" an Elizabethan might have exclaimed, because those procedures are most commonly laced with ambiguity and ambivalence. Chief among these uncertainties is the one that can be summed up with the following questions: "Are we 'buying' or are we 'selling'—and how do we go about drawing a line between those two functions?"

Let me begin on the most personal note and then move on to the "broader perspective."

I'm sitting in my office and interviewing for an important position one of the final candidates who has actually made it into the ranks of the half-dozen men and women on our "shortlist." The search committee, in this job-hungry age, was stunned by the number of applications submitted, but vigorous pruning has finally brought us— which definitely includes me—to this existential moment: me in one chair, the candidate in another, the two of us face-to-face.

Any fantasies I may have about serving as a polite but grand inquisitor swiftly melt away. The candidate had no sooner entered my office, after all, than I was trying to put him or her at ease. Offers of coffee or a soft drink were a matter of course. Inquiries regarding personal comfort, the adequacy of hotel accommodations, and mutual friends or acquaintances swiftly followed. And now I'm gripped by the awareness of just how much work and expense has in fact been expended in order to narrow the field to this "survivor"— and a handful of others whom I'll be meeting soon.

So I immediately fall into "selling" about as hard as I'm "buying"— and occasionally even harder. Do I want to stand accused, at some future point, of even the smallest act of commission or omission that might have lost us "the best of the lot"? Certainly not! And as I try to avoid any such dire fate, I, of course, run a most serious risk.

Not only in novels and films, after all, do we encounter nuances of personality that in fact "speak volumes" about the true shape of a human personality. That happens in real life as well, all of the time. But an interviewer needing to take seriously the hypothesis that "this one's the best of all" is not in optimal shape for knowing that he or she has, in fact, just encountered such a nuance. And if good manners and the projection of a good image lead the interviewer to skate right past it, then only the grim light of retrospect is likely—if this candidate is in fact hired—to reveal the awful mistake. As in a doomed marriage, the "small touch" or barely noticeable eccentricity ends up looming like Gibraltar or Everest.

How do I personally try to cope with this risk—rendered all the riskier, I should add, by the fact that interviews usually take place in the middle of a typical workday, with its nonstop procession of small and sometimes not-so-small triumphs, failures, stalemates, and painful compromises? I begin, before the candidate walks through my door, with some deep breaths and some conscious "calming down." I remind myself that what's about to happen is probably at least as important, where the long-term well-being of my university is concerned, as a meeting with a U.S. Senator or other widely known public figure and requires at least as much in the way of heightened attentiveness.

And I remind myself that the man or woman on the other side of the door has worked as hard to get here as we have worked to attract him or her. "It's our school and our payroll," is the crude essence of my little exercise in self-discipline. "I'm proud that it's pulling in such good people. And now I'm about to do my duty by deciding whether the one I'm about to interview is good *for us*."

That reflection, in turn, affects the content as well as the style of the conversation that follows. Only in my younger years as an administrator was I a bit shy about asking whether Fact X or Y or Z about my school might turn the candidate off. And to put the same matter in a more positive way, maturity in senior administrative positions has brought me to the point at which, in an interview situation, my tone pervasively implies: "Look, you and I are worldly sorts who understand a lot of what life's all about. That's why you and I are here, facing each other in this office. Now let's see whether you and this school are in fact a perfect, or only a partial, or possibly a disastrous 'match.' "

None of this makes me infallible, of course. But it certainly helps me to compensate for the role a university president is so often required to play these days—that of his or her school's public "face" or "image," more politely referred to as "advocate" or "spokesperson." No matter how admirable the candidate may be, no matter how aglow with virtue and competence his or her record may seem, "buying," in these difficult times, must take precedence over "selling."

And these acts of self-discipline also help me to avoid the treacherous dynamics that are set off when any two people previously unknown to each other form a "dyad"—*even* in an interview situation, and *even* with a résumé or curriculum vitae on the table. The "chemistry" between them is exactly that. Molecules fly, subatomic particles of personality are interchanged, and the "situation," the "mix," takes on "a life of its own." It's especially urgent that the interviewer develop habits of running self-criticism that defend him or her against common and dysfunctional psychic mechanisms such as, for example, projection.

Much of what I've said so far can be extended to those other than the president of the university or college who are interviewing the candidates for a particular position. And much more advice, ranging from useful to priceless, can be gleaned from the admirable essays by the other contributors to this volume. Still to come in this concluding chapter, moreover, are some remarks of my own on specific interviewing pitfalls that need to be avoided, on the main themes that emerge from this book, and—backtracking somewhat on what I've just said about the preeminence of "buying" over "selling"—on the need for those working in institutions of higher education, be they faculty members or be they administrators, to overcome a specific and long-established academic bias. That bias is an unreasoning hostility, especially pernicious where the art of hiring is concerned, toward anything that smacks of "marketing" (alias "Madison Avenue," alias "advertising").

But first I want to pause and say, in a comment meant to cover the contents of this entire book, that the *sine qua non* for a successful "hire" is a feeling or sense that, if it exists, will pervade and transform—for the better—all of the details and processes involved: the feeling of *confidence*.

To say such a thing is to risk a charge of banality. But only consider the vision conjured up by Vice-President Stein in the opening paragraphs of his introduction:

> Consequently, the general result is that when an outstanding candidate is brought to the attention of the search committee, the first question raised is, "Why does somebody that good want to come to our institution?" . . . The interview [by the search committee then] becomes a forum for telling the candidate everything that is wrong with the institution and for airing all the grievances the members of the search committee have against the institution. It would appear to a casual observer that their charge was to do their very best to talk the candidate out of coming to *their* institution. [Italics added.]

All of us know what would happen to a search committee that committed such misdeeds in the profit-making sector of the American economy. Heads would roll! Terror-stricken would be the faces of those "called on the carpet"! Abrupt demotions and salary freezes would soon be regarded as benevolent outcomes by those at the receiving end of "discipline from above"!

Schools of higher education operate under a different set of assumptions, however, initially generated by faculty members with tenure, then insensibly extending themselves to the administrative ranks as well. And rather than just attribute such hiring behaviors (or counterbehaviors) to amateurishness and lack of experience, I myself would root their cause in the academic culture itself.

People who are socialized, by their studies and by the norms of their daily work lives, to be incessantly critical—and also to be, therefore, incessantly criticized and defensively *self-critical*—will indeed be prone to some bafflement when they receive the compliment of a job application from a highly qualified candidate. People who are socialized to such an incessant storm of criticism will perhaps also be prone to what so many observers and participants in academic life have called a culture of *envy,* one marked by gossip, of oft-expressed resentment, and brooding jealousy.

This is emphatically not to say that academic life is devoid of admirable qualities, including the ideal known as Truth, whose importance grows exponentially even as the nonacademic world becomes too often a world of "appearances," based on information that is so easily manipulated and distorted. But envy has an unfortunate side effect that eats away at the ability of those conducting a job search to speak, to their best candidates, the only language to which the latter are likely to respond—the language of *confidence.* For a highly qualified professional, "Join our winning team!" will have certain advantages, as an enticement, over "Why do you want to come *here,* of all places?"

Which brings me to my list of hiring pitfalls.

Failure to consult

Academic work lives are necessarily tugged in many directions. The sheer amount of reading and other preparation they can require, the mastery and analysis of data, are enough to make a good night's sleep a special occasional treat. It's all too easy, therefore, for those involved in hiring to assume—where attitudinal issues are concerned—that "we already *know* all that."

But the "chemistry" involved when anywhere from five or six to a dozen people are engaged in assessing candidates makes the dyad in the president's office that usually takes place toward the very end of the process look, in comparison, as simple as putting the chocolate in chocolate milk. The time for issues of mutual confidence to be discussed, for example, is *before* the candidate's arrival on campus. Any feelings to the effect of not deserving a worthy candidate need to be articulated and dealt with. ("Why don't we feel that this candidate's telling us how much we've *improved* our position in the academic marketplace?")

Anxiety over the possibility of "a failed search"

In a time of such budgetary pressure as is now being experienced by most schools of higher education, the need to draw a line under one search and to start an entirely new one is, of course, experienced by the participants as painful, "a confession of failure," and—if seen through hostile or envious eyes—a reflection on the competence of those involved.

So what else is new? Those who indicate their willingness to take part in a search, besides regarding such a role as a sign of confidence in their school, also need to internalize the awareness that it is a *risky* process, and all the more risky when money is tight and the ability to "meet payroll" not guaranteed by God. No level of expense is more protracted and painful than that inevitably posed by a "successful" candidate who turns out to be a very *unsuccessful* "hire."

Failure of those involved to understand our present legal context

In a simpler age than the one we confront right now, rejected candidates for an academic position went home. Today, all too frequently, some may go to their lawyers.

In a simpler age, search committees, once they went to work, could focus entirely on classical qualifications. Today, they must also focus on "new" issues of equity summed up for some by the term Affirmative Action. Those who find this principle a repugnant violation of academic ideals have no business serving on contemporary search committees or in any way taking part in the search process. And unless they are willing to personally share in the costs levied against their school if it loses a lawsuit over a personnel decision, they would be well-advised to keep even their opinions to themselves.

A university president complains about the academic department involved in a recent "hire": "Every one of them male, middle-aged, and Caucasian. Every one of the candidates on the 'shortlist' submitted to the administration—ditto. And when I complained, the answer I got was: 'Well, that's all we have in this department.' "

A universal truth long acknowledged is that like tends to hire like. Without necessarily resorting to extreme expedients, institutions of higher education need to see to it that search committees are attuned to life in the year 1992 rather than 1892. Reading the 1991 Civil Rights Act can be a bracing experience. At the same time, the political necessity of including on search committees a representative of every conceivable category of human beings—scholars of various disciplines or sub-specialties, students, alumni, and so forth—diminishes the chances of consensus on criteria or values and increases the risk that choices will reflect the relative power of competing self-interests.

Failure to take seriously applicants from outside academic life

Those within universities and colleges who attended graduate school or started administrative careers anytime between 1955 and 1980 often feel that the gap between the academy and "the world outside" is very wide—and possibly unbridgeable.

Right now, the fiscal carpet-bombing that has so many academicians scurrying for cover is mostly coming from that very same "outside"—including its state governors and state legislators, its federal officials, its inquisitive journalists, and the disenchanted general public that supports "all of the above."

Those who understand "enemy territory" might conceivably prove useful—might they not?—in assisting the cause known as Survival.

Failure to understand the position itself

Marked benefits tend to flow from the fact that a search committee includes people from different parts of the school doing the hiring. Perspectives are broadened, parochialism is guarded against, and the candidate is given a three-dimensional sense of the institution whose ranks he or she may soon be joining. This is not an argument, however, for the "Noah's Ark" committee.

But those benefits obtain only for the search committee whose members do their homework and familiarize themselves with a job that may be quite different from their own. Hiring is hard work. Those not inclined to work hard should volunteer for other tasks, if any.

I have left for last the profoundest pitfall of all.

The very nature of committees

How many of us have attended meetings, conferences, or conventions in the course of which a professor comments on the amount of his or her time that is swallowed up by "committee work"—and gets an enormous sympathetic groan from the audience? How many of us *haven't?*

Just as bad money drives out good, so the negative aspects of committee work—tedium, repetitiousness, the need of each and every participant to present (often at length) his or her opinions, and the problems posed by late arrivals and sporadic absentees—tend to encroach upon and even to overwhelm the task(s) with which the committee is charged. The fact that a committee, by definition, involves shared rather than individual responsibility—and that "no one is, therefore, responsible"—opens the door to patterns of abuse that, in popular parlance, make the very word *committee* "good for a cheap laugh."

And the fear of responsibility, as well as the alleged academic propensity for jaundice when confronted by high and possibly superior talent, has given search committees a reputation for ostensibly choosing "vanilla" candidates, those so entrenched in the lowest common denominator that they threaten no one and nothing—but can't *do* very much, either.

Talents often come with some personal eccentricities as well. A highly talented person, having experienced some recognition—enough to be taken seriously by the search committee of a respectable university or college—is likely to have developed a good deal of self-confidence as well, too much to "iron" himself or herself into a neutral "persona" incapable of giving, now and then, just a bit of offense to those more concerned with propriety than performance.

The search committee that eliminates talent on such grounds cannot be called functional in terms of today's academic realities.

Possible prevention and cures for afflictions like those I've just listed, when a committee is charged with a task as critical for the host institution as hiring, include (a) the *appointment* of a highly credentialled and highly skilled chairperson who knows how to keep even a committee on-target and is blessed with enough talent not to fear others with comparable personal endowments, and/or (b) a radical reversal of the conventional arrangement whereby the committee culls through all the applicants for a position and sends only a few names and dossiers to the administration.

Perhaps the president, assisted by one or two senior administrators, should do the culling, while the committee chooses from the half-dozen or so candidates on the *president's* "shortlist." One advantage of such a novel arrangement might well be speed—an important consideration these days, when the best candidates don't tend to "wait around" as offers from other schools come in. Another is the frequent need to deal with "special requests" from the best candidates for a position, like help in "placing" a spouse.

For busy administrators to make the time needed to review many dossiers isn't easy. But the rule holds for them as well: hiring is hard work. And at a time when the main issue facing most schools of higher education is the one known as Survival—when administrative ranks, moreover, are being steadily thinned as cutbacks actually cut ever more backs—administration is hard work, too.

SHARED CONCERNS AND CONCLUSIONS

"Every book has its own history," I wrote as I began this concluding chapter to *The Art of Hiring*—and every book with several contributors, not to mention two editors, is an experiment, too. Either the subject under discussion will "click" in the minds of the authors, and "click" in ways that interlock with and complement each other, or the publisher may well decide to write this particular project off. That is why Vice-President Stein and I held our collective breath as the individual chapters "came in" and were commensurately relieved to discover how very neatly they dovetailed—allowing, of course, for the personal touches, inevitable in writers of talent and authority, that we did nothing to discourage or to edit. Among the themes shared by more than one contributor:

- That the actual *costs* of the hiring process, especially when a search turns out to be protracted, can be staggering and must be taken into careful account—a fact that may encourage the use of search consultants, popularly known as "headhunters." In some particularly important observations, Judith Block McLaughlin stresses the perils that ensue, especially where the most qualified applicants are concerned, when they don't receive the acknowledgments, follow-ups, and ongoing communications they require and expect—"routine" though also "custom-tailored" tasks that search consultants perform as a matter of course. (And according to Lewis C. Solmon and Cheryl L. Fagnano, the hiring of faculty "will become both more difficult and more expensive over the next decade and a half.")

- That certain unique features of academic life—chiefly the limited power and authority of the "chief executive officer"—severely compromise the hiring process and the likelihood of its success. The filling of major administrative posts in particular, Joseph F. Kauffman emphasizes, has often become contentious in ways never before imagined. And in such a counterhierarchical atmosphere, Donald W. Jugenheimer notes, "There is no such thing as a secret deal: somebody will find out, and the greater the necessity of keeping a deal secret, the greater the problems created when the deal becomes known." Milton Greenberg's summary: "A measure of distrust, even a little hatred between management and labor, appears to be part of the human condition, but only in academe do the workers play a major role in choosing their own disliked managers."

- That what a job candidate is exposed to, when he or she comes to campus, is not just the structured interview-and-assessment process but the school's wall-to-wall "culture," also known as its full reality. To quote Milton Greenberg again: "I have been amazed at how much 'dirt' a candidate can uncover in the course of a day or two on a strange campus." The need to have one's house in order, if one wants to hire the very best people available, thus extends to the *entire* house—not just the room(s) in which interviews are conducted.

- That the ideal combination of qualities in a specific search process is an impeccable handling of "bureaucratic" details *and* "the personal touch." M. Fredric Volkmann notes the potency of a phone call as opposed to a written communication, and the importance of speaking with a top finalist's supervisor. Joseph F. Kauffman emphasizes the importance of the president's personal involvement in hiring: "The president, and especially the attitude and morale of the president, will tend to attract or discourage those being recruited to be either a serious candidate or to actually accept an offer of an appointment."

- That the changes of recent years have mandated greatly enhanced sensitivity to the needs of female and minority-group candidates, as well as spouses and "dual-career couples." Marian J. Swoboda, together with Sue A. Blanshan and E. Gordon Gee, communicates the arrival of what I myself would call a "changed organizational culture," one that, in Swoboda's words, can make hiring committees "feel internally motivated, rather than externally pressured, to seek diverse candidates." At the same time, those who set up these committees need to make certain that they are not "weighted" in ways that cut in the opposite direction.

- That the ostensible "line" between the academic and business worlds has become considerably more porous. The same bad economic news is crashing in on both these days. Lessons can be learned, by those engaged in hiring for a school of higher education, from the hiring practices employed in the corporate sector of the economy. "Because it is a continuing process," Ronald H. Stein and Ronald Caruso note, businesses seek to have hiring "run as efficiently as possible. Essential to that efficient functioning is self-knowledge. A company or institution must recognize what it can achieve and admit what it cannot; in addition, it must also know how the individuals it recruits are to serve its present and future needs." As a counterbalance, Solmon and Fagnano, having catalogued the escalating expenditures and declining popularity that now confront our universities and colleges, emphasize that these "make hiring as much an art as a business decision."

THE MARKETING CONFRONTATION
PAR EXCELLENCE

In the late 1950s, when I myself was an undergraduate, it might well have been termed an "existential" moment. A man or a woman whose career is at stake (in our supremely career-conscious age) faces, in a hiring context, those who regard the future of their *school* as being at stake. Antennae are up, poised to receive even the smallest hints of "an attitude" or "a gaffe." Images are being projected with an intensity and an instantaneity that even the electronic media cannot match. And be it right or wrong, on target or utterly misguided, interpretation pours through the minds of all concerned like an intrapsychic Niagara in quest of its ultimate repose.

That everyone involved on both sides of the negotiation is "trying to do the right thing" goes without saying. Each has given thought to the process itself. Each must face himself or herself, his or her conscience, when, for better or worse, "it's all over." And each has, of course, read *The Art of Hiring* and paused for at least a moment over the final sentences of chapter five, M. Fredric Volkmann's "What to Look for in a Candidate":

> Unfortunately, no matter how many safeguards and procedures are carefully followed, you have no guarantee that the right decision has been made. That comes only from a little luck and solid management principles employed in the initial experiences of the successful candidate in your new position.

And what more is there to say? Only—in my own opinion— what follows!

There was a time, not too many years ago, when any hint of "marketing" was regarded, in the self-respecting segments of the academic world, as roughly analogous to the Black Plague in medieval times. Indeed, the status hierarchy of that bygone age was ruled by institutions of such antiquity and respectability—not to mention large capital endowments—that they would ponder for a decade or two any suggestion of perhaps adding a second color to the cover of the catalogue. "*They* come to us—we don't go to *them*" might have summarized the attitude they projected toward, or over the heads of, their ever-so-envious inferiors further down the pyramid—

and they meant that attitude to apply to candidates seeking jobs as well as to students seeking admission.

Times have changed considerably, and few informed eyebrows will shoot heavenward when I refer to the hiring situation as one that involves a complex and lightning-fast interplay of marketing strategies and interpretations, as both the school and the applicant probe and project their respective "appearances."

But marketing, as companies in the profit-making sector of the American economy learned—or should have learned!—long ago, cuts in two directions. Those in charge of doing it carry the company's "best face" to consumers. They must also, if they are conscientious, bring into the company the news of whether and how that "best face" is being received, which in turn has everything to do with the perceived quality and utility of the company's products or services.

Marketing personnel, in other words, serve as "change-agents" *within* the company at the same time that they serve as "broadcasters" to those who must buy what the company is offering to sell.

And that, to an ever-increasing extent, is true of those within our schools of higher education—those responsible for admissions, for development, for investments, *and* for hiring faculty, administrators, and staff, whose professional lives are centered on various types of marketing work.

When Stanford University announces its newfound concern with regard to the teaching of undergraduates, and when a host of other "flagship" schools publicly express their regrets with regard to some of the items they have billed to federal funding agencies as "research overhead," we are seeing and hearing them respond to marketing considerations of this kind. Reforms are being self-imposed—as is so typical of human nature and human history—when to do otherwise would be a form of organizational suicide. The flow of information from the "outside" leads to substantive conversion on the "inside."

And the same is true, I would like to suggest as I conclude both my chapter and this book, of the art of hiring. The hiring process seeks to find the "best man or woman possible," to produce a true "marriage" of the right candidate with the right position, and to benefit, ultimately, both the candidate being considered and the school doing the considering. But if it is to serve its optimal function(s), then the art of hiring needs to be artfully applied. Search committees and search personnel need to let their schools' senior administrators know what candidates for jobs explicitly or implicitly report to be the strengths and weaknesses they have uncovered, and that applies to those hired as well as to those who either refuse or are refused the positions in which they were originally interested. And if that still seems to some of those working in the academic world as a humble if not humiliating stance to take, well, let them reflect on the present decade as one that is teaching us all, both inside and outside the groves of academe, how vulnerable we all are and how humble we sometimes have to be.

Contributors

SUE A. BLANSHAN is Dean at Hartford College for Women.

RONALD CARUSO is President of R. H. Caruso and Company, Incorporated, an executive firm specializing in equipment financing industry and related financial services, both domestic and international.

CHERYL L. FAGNANO is Vice-President for Administration and Educational Programs at the Milken Institute for Job and Capital Formation.

E. GORDON GEE is President of Ohio State University.

MILTON GREENBERG is Provost of the American University, Washington, D.C.

DONALD W. JUGENHEIMER is Chairman, Department of Communications and Speech at Fairleigh Dickinson University.

JOSEPH F. KAUFFMAN is Professor Emeritus in the Department of Higher Education at the University of Wisconsin at Madison and formerly Executive Vice-President of the University of Wisconsin system and President of the University of Rhode Island.

JUDITH BLOCK MCLAUGHLIN is Lecturer in Higher Education in Administration, Planning, and Social Policy at Harvard Graduate School of Education.

LEWIS C. SOLMON is President of the Milken Institute for Job and Capital Formation.

RONALD H. STEIN is Vice-President for University Relations at the State University of New York at Buffalo and Associate Professor, Graduate School of Education.

MARIAN J. SWOBODA is Assistant to the President for Equal Opportunity Programs and Policy Studies for the University of Wisconsin system.

STEPHEN JOEL TRACHTENBERG is President of George Washington University and Professor of Public Administration.

M. FREDRIC VOLKMANN is Vice-Chancellor for Public Affairs at Washington University in St. Louis.